THE PAY-PER-CLICK Playbook

STEVE TENERIELLO

AHM

ANCHOR HOUSE MEDIA

AnchorHousePrint.com

Sales and Service Media Group, Inc.

Published By: Sales and Service Media Group, Inc., Anchor House Media, Boston, Massachusetts

Author: Steven Teneriello
Editor: Bethany Thomas
Editor: Bridget O'Brien
Cover Design: Kostis Pavlou
Interior Design: Kevin Lee

Anchor House Media
PO Box 462
Amesbury, MA 01913

Library of Congress Control Number: 2019915685
Teneriello, Steven M. 1982-

To my beautiful wife Allison and my children Madeline Rose and William Joseph. You inspire and motivate me everyday. I'm truly a lucky guy to have your unconditional love and support. I love you.

Table of Contents

WELCOME TO THE ONLINE ADVERTISING GAME

SECTION 2: THE PROVEN AD COPY FORMULA

SECTION 3: THE GOOGLE AD BLUEPRINT

SECTION 4: GOOGLE AD EXTENSIONS

HALF-TIME

SECTION 5: LANDING PAGE FUNDAMENTALS

SECTION 6: LANDING PAGE PERFORMANCE

SECTION 7: CAMPAIGN TYPES

7th Inning Stretch

SECTION 8: PAY-PER-CLICK PERFORMANCE MANAGEMENT

SECTION 9: FIXING COMMON PAY-PER-CLICK PROBLEMS

SECTION 10: CHOOSING THE RIGHT GOOGLE PARTNER

Download The PPC Scorecard and Receive Exclusive Access to Additional Resources

READ THIS FIRST

Just to say thanks for reading my book, I would like to give you the PPC Scorecard that goes along with each chapter **PLUS** exclusive access to tools, resources and training.

Go To: registerppcbook.com to access the materials.

Acknowledgement

This book would not be here without the help of Bethany Thomas, Bridget O'Brien, and Kevin Lee. Your dedication to this project allowed my vision to become a reality. I appreciate every hour spent working alongside this talented group.

At the same time, I'd like to thank my entire team at AdMachines. Without them, I would not have had the time to focus on writing. Their hard work did not go unnoticed as I spent many hours away creating this book. Thank you.

Last, but not least, I would like to thank my clients. Without you, I would have nothing to write about.

Pre-Game

If you want to take control of your lead cost, generate higher quality leads, improve response rates, and bring in traffic that turns into revenue then you need an optimized and well run pay-per-click account. But where do you start when the world of Google is so large? You need to start with a solid game plan that guides you to the places where you can make a real change and get results. You need a coach who's going to bring you through their playbook, one that's packed with years of experience and proven plays that score big for your business.

Now, I wrote this book for two reasons. First, it started as a training manual for new hires at my company. I wanted them to see how we manage accounts and what we expect in Google account management. It's not a traditional how-to guide. It really is like seeing inside my personal playbook and taking apart the intricacies of the best performing ad campaigns.

Second, I wrote it because I wanted to help local business owners take control of pay-per-click campaigns that have flatlined for whatever reason. It's designed in a way where you can implement a play and see results in the same business cycle. These are tips and strategies that I know work, and I wanted to make them accessible.

You may have been trying to get your pay-per-click campaign into a winning rhythm but found little success. Or maybe you've been working with a PPC Manager who's left you on the sidelines. In order to get a lower cost per click, better position and exposure, and a direct line to your best customers your account needs daily, weekly, and monthly management. Think of these as the various plays a coach uses in a game. Each one highlights the strength of a certain player; keywords, ad copy, messaging, ad position, bids, technology, new advertising markets etc. These are your star players that push the account forward to success. But they need to be coached and put through drills in order to perform on game day. You'll see firsthand how my system takes out of control accounts and places them into a steady program.

In *The Pay Per Click Playbook* You're Going To Learn:

- How To Easily Identify and Eliminate Wasted Ad Spend

- How To Get More High Quality Leads Without Increasing Your Budget

- How To Use Google's NEW Targeting Features To Connect with the Right Audiences

- Proven Ways To Improve Response and Lead Conversion Rates

- How To Achieve Greater Positioning and Gain More Exposure

- How To Ethically Spy on Your Competitors and Identify Weaknesses in Their PPC Strategy

- How To Identify Broken Areas in Your Campaigns and Fix Them

- Plus Free Downloads, Tools & Resources Along With Exclusive Videos You Can Access to Improve Your Pay-Per-Click Performance

Pregame is over. It's time to crack open the playbook and start taking your ad account success to the next level.

—

*"You know what my favorite
Super Bowl ring is? The next one."*

-Tom Brady

SECTION #1
KEYWORDS

TIPS, TOOLS, REPORTS, AND RESOURCES TO IMPLEMENT THE FUNDAMENTALS OF GOOGLE ADS.

You'll Discover the Keyword Blocking and Tackling Skills to Size up Your Market, Identify New Sales Opportunities, Enhance Lead Quality, Prevent Bleeding Budgets, Get In Front of the Right Audience, Set a Proper Budget and Get a Read on Your Competition.

PLAY #1 | The One Report Your PPC Manager Doesn't Want You to See - The Search Terms Report

Play Action:

Identify Keywords Draining Your Budget and Block Them to Prevent Future Wasted Ad Spend.

Google is one of the most transparent advertising solutions out there that gives you all of the necessary information you need to control your outcome. You just need to know where to go to access this information and how to apply it to make impactful performance improvements. In this book, I'm going to help you identify these areas and what you should do to get an immediate result

With that said, one of the most useful reports to help you immediately stop wasteful ad spending is the Search Terms Report. This one report can make a huge impact on your account because it shows you everything you paid for and how the account has been managed. If you've been working with an outside PPC agency and you feel like your account has been on cruise control, there's a good chance this report will really catch your PPC manager with their pants down.

I have personally taken over "**set and forget**" accounts and seen how poorly managed they were more times that I can remember. It's certainly an eye-opening report; one than can turn your stomach inside out once you see hundreds of clicks start to add up to *thousands of dollars* in wasted ad spend that could have been avoided if the account were properly managed.

The search terms report provides you with a complete and detailed audit trail of all the keywords that triggered an ad and resulted in a click on your account. It's essentially Google's accounting system. Here you are able to identify top performing keywords, keywords that need further optimization, and keywords that completely drained your budget. It's a best practice to review this report every day to sort through the keywords and take necessary improvement actions. If you stay on top of the report and manage it properly, you'll see your account performance improve every day. This is PPC 101. The basics. The foundation of any strong pay-per-click program.

When you look at the search terms report for the first time, you want to drill into any keywords triggering an ad that do not make sense for your business. Take those bad fit terms and use them to block future non-relevant traffic from draining your budget by implementing a negative keyword list. Don't worry, we'll take a closer look at negative keywords up ahead.

The search terms report is available at any time and is super easy to access. All you have to do is:

1. Log into your Google Ads Account

2. Go to the keywords section

3. Click on the search terms tab

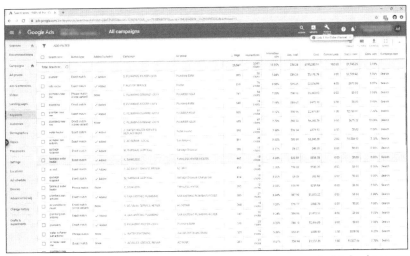

fig. 2-1: Search term report

From your keywords report, you'll be able to see an entire history of all the keywords that resulted in a click by date range. If you're paying close attention to this report and take action on it you'll start to see higher quality leads, better opportunities, and an improved return on spend.

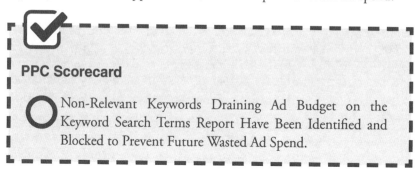

PPC Scorecard

O Non-Relevant Keywords Draining Ad Budget on the Keyword Search Terms Report Have Been Identified and Blocked to Prevent Future Wasted Ad Spend.

Play #1 / One Report Your PPC Manager Doesn't Want You To See

PLAY #2 | How To Enhance Lead Quality & Capture More Traffic With Broad Match Modified Keywords

Play Action:

Use Broad Match Modified Keywords to Decrease Bleeding Budgets, Get in Front of the Right Audience, and Grow Qualified Traffic.

If you want to cast a wide net, drive qualified traffic, and attract your best customers then using broad match modified keywords are your best option. Broad match modifiers give you more control over the quality of traffic in your campaigns compared to traditional broad keywords. At the same time, broad match modified keywords are flexible and will help you capture more search volume because they are less restrictive compared to phrase match keywords.

Broad match modified keywords include the exact keyword, with other terms before or after your keyword. Before broad match modified keywords were introduced you would have to worry about budget bleeding and poor quality traffic with traditional broad keywords. This is because broad keywords are only as effective as your negative keyword list. At the same time you would have to kill yourself thinking about a hundred different ways people might search when it came to implementing phrase match keywords.

Think of broad match modified keywords as a hybrid between broad keywords and phrase match keywords that deliver you high-quality traffic without having to worry about a ton of negative keywords or search phrases. You'll know if you are using broad match modified keywords when you see your keywords marked with plus signs.

For instance, if you were a contractor with the broad match modified keywords +remodeling +contractor, Google will only serve your ad to people who use these specific words in their search along with any other words before and after them.

If a homeowner searched **contractor renovation** on Google your ad would not appear in this example because the search did not include the word remodeling, however if the homeowner searched **local contractor remodeling reviews** the ad would appear because the search term includes both remodeling and contractor.

 Steve's PPC Breakdown

Here's an example:

Goal: A local plumbing company wanting to generate water heater replacement leads. The broad match modified keyword:
+water +heater +replacement

Example search that will trigger an ad: *water heater replacement prices.* This search includes all keywords water, heater, and replacement. The word prices can appear in any order as long as all of the initial keywords are included in the search.

Example search that **will not** trigger an ad: *water heater prices* This search does not include the search term replacement.

Here's another example:

Goal: A local optometrist wanting to generate new patients wanting an eye exam. The broad match modified keyword: **+eye +doctor +near**

Example searches that will trigger an ad: eye doctor near Boston, eye doctor near me, reviewed eye doctor near me. All of these terms include eye, doctor, and near.

Example searches that will not trigger an ad: eye specialist near Boston, eye surgeon near me, reviewed optometrist near me. All of these terms did not include all of the keywords.

Fill Up Your Sales Pipeline With High Quality Leads

With broad match modifiers, you have control over the type of leads you're receiving. It's the ultimate time-saver that prevents you from having to sift through (or answer calls from) people who aren't the right fit for your products or services. As your sales pipeline becomes more tailored to what you're looking for your CTR (or click through rate) and conversion rate will also improve.

Broad match modifiers are simple to set up and the pay-off is big. You can add a modifier to an existing keyword by simply editing that word and adding the + prefix without any spaces. By decreasing the junk from broad searches (searches that don't match the buyers you're looking for) you'll be saving money and a lot of frustration dealing with low quality leads. Broad match modifiers give you greater control over how you spend your budget.

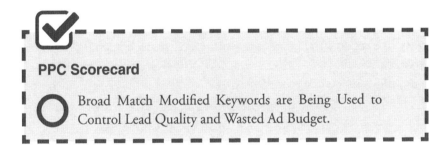

PPC Scorecard

Broad Match Modified Keywords are Being Used to Control Lead Quality and Wasted Ad Budget.

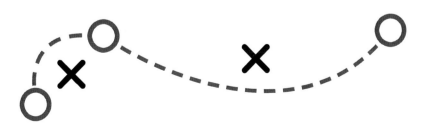

Play #2 / How To Enhance Lead Quality & Capture More Traffic

PLAY #3

A Simple Step-by-Step Daily System to Improve Keyword Performance

Play Action:

Implement the PPC Accounting System to Focus on Top Performing Keywords, Troubleshoot Underperforming Keywords and Eliminate Keywords Draining Your Ad Budget.

Every business owner has an accounting system to keep track of sales, expenses, and profits. I'm sure you have your very own way of doing accounting. If you own a big business, you pay a bookkeeper to track all the financial activity day-to-day. You can apply the same accounting principles to your pay-per-click advertising. Although as Google is a powerful tool to reach your target audience with direct response marketing, it's also a sophisticated financial system.

Pay-Per-Click (or PPC) accounting is the practice of reviewing the daily activity in your account and making financial decisions that will impact your outcome. Looking at the keyword search terms report, you can see which keyword triggered an ad and what you paid for that click. Think of keywords as stock in your portfolio. Some keywords are going to deliver consistent returns, others will deliver results some of the time, you'll have many that never deliver a result at all and some keywords that don't make sense or are not relevant to your sales goals that are costing you money.

The most common non-relevant keyword categories I see are:

- O   Keywords triggered based on a competitor search.
- X   Keywords triggering ads outside your local service area.
- O   Keywords triggered by searchers who searched keywords in your campaigns, but those keywords did not match the outcome you wanted.

The Pay-Per-Click Accounting Checklist

So where do you begin? How does one perform PPC accounting? You start by evaluating all the search terms you come across. The ones that resulted in a lead you'll want to keep and prioritize. You'll want to isolate these keywords and focus your ad dollars on these terms because they are proven winners, delivering consistent results.

Next, take a look at the keywords that make sense and are core to your business but did not produce a result or may have produced a result at one time and are no longer effective. You may have received clicks but no leads, or lots of search impressions with limited click activity, or perhaps you're getting plenty of clicks without conversions. You know these terms are extremely relevant to your business, yet they are not producing the results you expected.

Here you can troubleshoot these terms in an effort to improve performance:

- O   Change ad copy to improve response rates.
- X   Test bid rates in an effort to improve the position.
- O   Adjust your timing to ensure your ads are running at optimal search volume times.
- O   Verify your location settings are accurate.
- X   Check your device-specific bidding and position.
- X   Make sure you are sending prospects to a landing page that matches your offer.

Finally, you want to evaluate the keywords that drain your budget. These are one-off keywords that come from left field and cost you a click but

Steve's PPC Breakdown

Let's take a look at a local air conditioner repair rompany. There's a good chance they want to bid and trigger an ad for the terms: *ac repair, ac service,* and *air conditioner repair.* They most likely do not want to trigger ads for *Toyota ac repair, Chevy Tahoe ac service* and *RV air conditioner repair* because they do not work on vehicles.

These are the types of opportunities you'll identify in the PPC accounting procedure.

It's important to remember that whether or not the keyword triggered the result you were looking for, you still paid for it. You own the click and can't return it.

Luckily, you've paid for the opportunity to take corrective action so that it doesn't happen again. If you're willing to dedicate 20-30 minutes of focus daily to your keywords there's a great way to get a handle on keywords that aren't producing the results you want.

The practice of daily PPC accounting will help you take a closer look at your account and start moving it in the right direction. By improving lead quality with a daily PPC accounting regiment, you'll become more cost-efficient because your ad dollars will be focused on the places that deliver you results.

PPC Scorecard

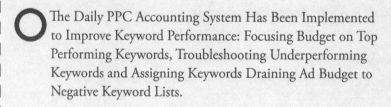 The Daily PPC Accounting System Has Been Implemented to Improve Keyword Performance: Focusing Budget on Top Performing Keywords, Troubleshooting Underperforming Keywords and Assigning Keywords Draining Ad Budget to Negative Keyword Lists.

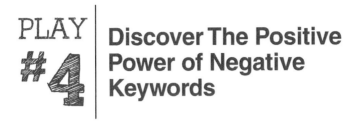

PLAY
#4

Discover The Positive Power of Negative Keywords

Play Action:

Brainstorming Exercise:

Develop a Comprehensive List of the Keywords You Don't Want Triggering Ads to Help You Control Lead Quality and Prevent Wasted Ad Spend.

If you want to control your lead quality, eliminate wasted ad spend, and prevent the wrong opportunities from coming into your sales pipeline you'll want to implement a complete list of negative keywords.

Negative keywords are the terms you use that basically tell Google *"Hey, don't serve my ad here."* When it comes to adding negative keywords to your account the rule of thumb is the more the merrier. The main reason you want as many negative keywords as possible is that they deflect bad traffic that impacts budget and lead quality. In simplified terms, bad traffic can be defined as: the people you're spending money advertising to who won't become future customers. Implementing comprehensive negative keyword lists on your campaigns will save you from wasting your ad budget.

How do you begin the process identifying negative keywords? The best place to start is to brainstorm and create lists. Think of all the scenarios where someone may type something into Google that is really close to what you do, but doesn't quite make sense to serve your ads. I'll give you some examples so you can see what this could look like.

O   List of competitors in your area.

○
✗ List of parts or common supplies used in your industry. Think of the components that you would search for, not your customers.

List of vendors or suppliers in your area or industry.

○ List of cities where you do not want traffic close to your area. Note: If you set up Google's geo-locations you can still attract out of area traffic from people work in your service area, but do not live there.

✗ List of early stage buying interest. If your goal is to run a conservative campaign you can block early stage buying activity. For example, your local kitchen and bath remodeling company may want to block traffic from people looking for ideas, pictures or inspiration.

✗ List of questions. Blocking the terms who, what, where, when, why, and how might make sense if you want to prevent people who are unsure about exactly what they are looking for.

○ List of close matches. In the following example you'll notice a pharmaceutical company offering knee pain medicine running an ad for the term "*knee replacement surgery dog.*" By simply adding the term "dog" to the negative lists, this ad would not have triggered.

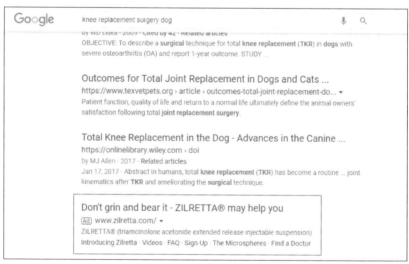

fig. 4-1: Negative keywords

When done correctly, adding negative keywords is a daily practice. By whittling down and optimizing your keyword portfolio you'll really be 'tightening the belt' so to speak as you determine who should be seeing your ads.

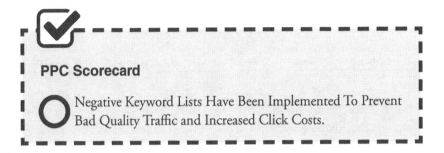

PPC Scorecard

◯ Negative Keyword Lists Have Been Implemented To Prevent Bad Quality Traffic and Increased Click Costs.

PLAY #5 | How To Track and Measure Revenue Performance at the Keyword Level

Play Action:

Technical Setup: Start Tracking the Performance of Individual Keywords by Integrating Google Ads with Your Landing Pages, Google Analytics and Call Tracking Software.

John Wannamaker, who founded the first department store in Philadelphia in 1861, coined the phrase *"Half the money I spend on advertising is wasted; the trouble is, I don't know which half."*

You've probably heard this saying along the way if you've been in business for a while, and if you haven't, you heard it here first! The saying basically means you know your advertising is working, but you are unable to measure the parts that drive in revenue. This still holds true to this day 150+ years later. There are a lot of advertisers out there who throw money at Google without understanding the parts that impact revenue performance. They just know it works.

Like I mentioned earlier, the beauty of Google Ads is you can control your outcome because you have all of the transparent information you need to make decisions. The most basic and fundamental part of Google is paying for keywords, so wouldn't you want to know which keywords are generating leads and which ones aren't?

You can get this information by setting up keyword-level conversion tracking.

Keyword level conversion tracking is the practice of tracking leads as conversions at the keyword level within Google Ads. This setup allows you to attribute lead generation credit to the keywords that triggered the ads, giving you complete visibility into which keywords drive in results and which ones do not. This is important because it shows exactly where your budget is working and not working. You will be able to measure your advertising success with accuracy.

It's a technical setup that requires integrating your call tracking solution with Google Analytics along with your landing pages so they post information to your Google Ads account. Think of it as a system closing the loop from initial click to the phone call or form submission. It's an industry best practice that shows your individual keyword performance.

How it works:

- ○ Your call tracking provider will have a website script that needs to be installed on your landing pages.

- ○ You install what's called a 'keyword pool.' This is a list of phone lines that track the unique activity of each user.

- ○ As soon as someone clicks your ad and lands on your landing page, the phone line and script plants a cookie on the user's browser which assigns them to a unique call tracking line from the keyword pool.

- ○ This cookie relays all the user's real time information: the keyword that triggered the ad, the unique ad copy, the device they are using, along with any other factors you've chosen to receive intelligence on.

- ○ When the user calls the assigned call tracking line, the system will post the keyword data back to Google Ads issuing lead conversion credit for that keyword.

With this information, you not only get the actual cost per lead direct from Google Ads, but you'll know which specific keywords drive revenue. You'll gain a deeper understanding of your ROI as it relates to keyword performance. Keyword level conversion tracking is the best practice to effectively track individual keywords and dial in on your performance. Without it, you're just guessing at what's impacting overall revenue performance.

Play #5 / How To Track and Measure Revenue Performance

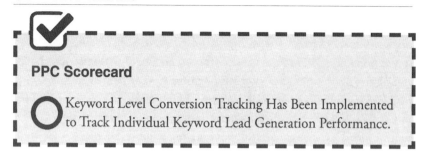

PPC Scorecard

Keyword Level Conversion Tracking Has Been Implemented to Track Individual Keyword Lead Generation Performance.

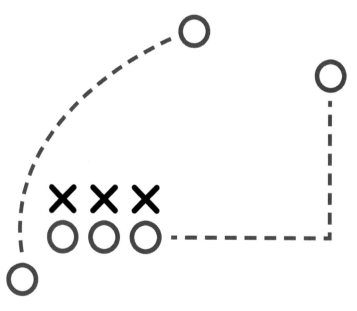

Play #5 / How To Track and Measure Revenue Performance

PLAY #6

How To Achieve a Higher Ad Position Without Spending More on Clicks

Play Action:

Evaluate Individual Keyword Quality Scores And Take Corrective Action On Ads And Landing Pages To Increase Your Ranking.

Unlike SEO (where Google does not provide you with a formal playbook or set of rules to optimize your website so you can grow your organic presence) Google does provide you with a system to improve your PPC performance. Part of that system includes your Google Quality Score or QS.

QS is a measurement of the overall combined effectiveness of your ads, keywords, and landing pages. These are the basics of Google Ads- your 3-legged stool. The higher the quality, the lower you'll pay for clicks. You'll also achieve better ad positioning with a higher quality score. This is Google's way of rewarding you for delivering value to searchers. That's why it's important to make sure that you design your campaigns with the searchers in mind. Your goal should always be to provide them with a highly consistent experience from the initial search, to clicking on your ad, to viewing your landing page.

Reasons Why Quality Score Exists

O   First and foremost, Google wants a relevant experience for all of its users- the 5.6 billion searchers each and every day.

○ Once upon a time you could "ride the news" with Google AdWords- running an ad in front of an audience who might be interested in the latest celebrity scandal or news event. You could capture their eyes just like a billboard, getting in front of a lot of viewers, showing them an ad for life insurance, or even dog food if you wanted, even though it was not relevant to their search.

○ It forces you to do the work. You need ad copy that has been well thought out along with a landing page that delivers a great experience for each and every product and service.

How To Look Up Quality Score

To see your quality score, all you have to do is go to the keyword section within your account. Here your keywords are ranked on a scale of 1-10, with 10 being optimal performance. At the same time, Google will provide you with a rating for both your landing page experience and your ad copy experience. This rating will come in the form of 'below average, average, or above average.' This lets you know where you need to focus your attention and make improvements.

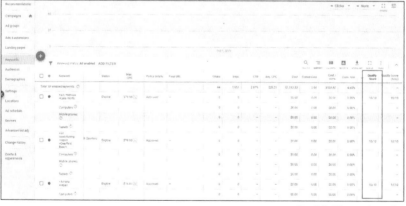

fig. 6-2: Keywords section

At the same time you can go to the keywords section and add in quality score and historical quality score in the keyword columns. I find this view to be easier to read. I'm also able to see the historical changes over time to monitor improvements to the score.

Play #6 / How To Achieve a Higher Ad Position Without Spending More

How To Improve Quality Score

It may sound simple, but when it comes to improving your ad copy and quality score one of the best ways is to make sure you've included the keyword in your ad copy. You'll also want to have a number of variations of your ad being tested. Lastly, be sure to have an attractive and compelling offer. This will help you improve your CTR (or click-through rate) and ultimately your overall score. It's vital that your landing page has the **EXACT** components of your Google Ad as well.

 Steve's PPC Breakdown

I wouldn't stress out about quality score for all of your keywords. You may have a handful of keywords that will always have a low quality score no matter what you do. These are often single broad keywords that drive in a lot of traffic. Typically in the larger spending accounts I manage I'm going to have what I would consider a traffic kicker campaign. Here I drive in a ton of traffic and refine the terms as they come in.

When you intentionally do this there is no way around a low quality score because the looser you manage a keyword, the lower the overall CTR. However, the benefit of this lower quality score is the extra traffic you generate. Quality Score doesn't really matter when your lead conversion is strong.

PPC Scorecard

Low Quality Score Keywords Have Been Identified and Action is Being Taken to Optimize Ads and Improve Landing Pages in an Effort to Increase Quality Score Performance.

How To Properly Manage Top Performing Keywords

Play Action:

Identify Your Best Keywords and Create Single Keyword Ad Groups to Achieve Top Performance.

If you're not familiar with the Pareto principle (also known as the 80/20 rule) it states that in life 80% of the effects come from 20% of the causes. In terms of the distribution of wealth, the richest 20% of people have more wealth than the other 80%. In terms of your smartphone, there's a good chance you have a bunch of apps installed but only regularly use 20% of them. You can find this principle everywhere in life… business, sports, etc. You can even find it in Google Ads.

Out of all the keywords you manage, your top 20% are going to drive in 80% of the performance. Knowing this, you'll want to manage your account as such with a practice known as S.K.A.G.S (or single keyword ad groups). S.K.A.G.S is a method whereby you focus most of your attention on the top 20% of your keywords. You isolate them and place single keywords into their own dedicated ad groups within the campaign.

This structure makes it easier to manage, in turn helping you improve your quality score. It allows you to clean out your keyword closet by eliminating your low volume, non-impression capturing keywords. It helps you get the full impact of your best keywords by creating their very own ads, fine-tuning and optimizing them one at a time and giving them the budget they deserve.

The only downside to S.K.A.G management is the time, effort, and energy it takes to set up and manage. Rest assured, this time is well invested. It will help you get control and achieve much higher performance.

Think of S.K.A.G.S as managing a sales team. If you've ever managed more than a handful of sales reps you probably have one that really knocks it out of the park. He's the guy who gets the Glengarry Glen Ross leads *(and if you don't that saying you probably haven't seen the movie...)* The closer in any smart sales team typically gets the best leads because you trust that rep to close the deal.

S.K.A.G.S do the same thing. That keyword is going to perform when you give it love and attention by feeding it budget.

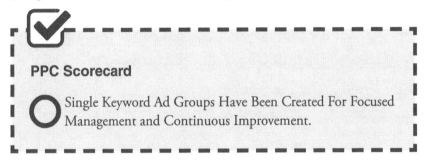

PPC Scorecard

Single Keyword Ad Groups Have Been Created For Focused Management and Continuous Improvement.

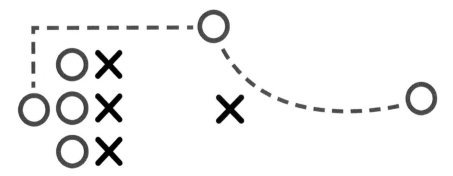

Play #7 / How To Properly Manage Top Performing Keywords

PLAY #8 | 5 Ways to Determine How Much Traffic Your Competition is Taking Away From You

Play Action:

See How Much Traffic Your Ads are Getting Compared to Your Competition, Identify Opportunities to Increase Market Share and Lead Volume.

Have you ever wondered how many times your ad is viewed compared to your competitors? What percentage of the time your ad was clicked on compared to everyone else? How about how much traffic your own ad received in the top spot compared to the next guy?

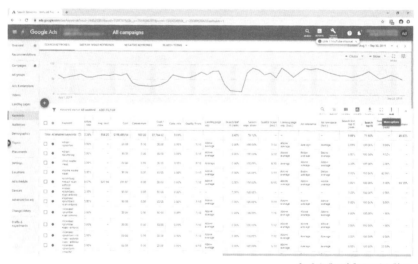

fig. 8-1: Search Impression Share

You're in luck. There are a number of keyword analysis tools you can view right at the keyword level telling you the exact answers to these questions. Let's drill into them.

1. **Impression share** is the percentage of impressions your ads received compared to the total number of impressions they could have received. Impression share gives you a read on your market, telling you how much search opportunity is available. Targeting settings, approval statuses, and quality score are all factors used to determine your eligible impressions.

   Ways to Improve Impression Share:

   O Increase your budget.

   ✗ Adjust your bidding.

   O Improve your ad copy.

2. **Search lost top impression share due to rank** is a metric that estimates how often your ads didn't show anywhere above the organic search results due to poor rank. This is determined by your bid relative to your competitors as well as your ad quality. If conversion is low or non-existent and you want action from this keyword you can increase your bid and improve your ad copy.

3. **Search top impression share** are the impressions you've received in the top location above the organic results compared to the number of impressions you were eligible to receive in the top location.

4. **Search absolute top impression share** are the impressions you've received in the top location (i.e the very first ad slot above the organic results) divided by the estimated number of impressions you were eligible to receive in the top location. Search absolute top impression share basically tells you what percentage of the time your ad is the first one people see. Testing your ad in number of spots helps you find the right balance of traffic and leads at the best and most efficient price.

5. **Click share** is the estimated percentage of all the achievable clicks you received and gives you insights into the additional click volume you can capture. Google will analyze all the ad auctions from the day and include all the auctions your ad showed in including the auctions where your ad competed but did not show. **Click share is useful because it's a great metric to use when determining the appropriate spending level and/or budget in your market.**

By learning and using these 5 simple reporting tools you'll be on your way to a more cost friendly budget, higher quality leads, and a greater understanding of where you stand amongst your competitors.

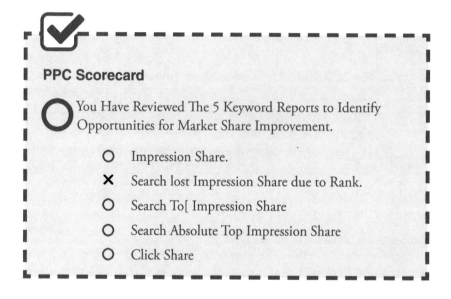

PPC Scorecard

O You Have Reviewed The 5 Keyword Reports to Identify Opportunities for Market Share Improvement.

    O Impression Share.

    ✕ Search lost Impression Share due to Rank.

    O Search To[Impression Share

    O Search Absolute Top Impression Share

    O Click Share

PLAY #9 How To Get X-Ray Vision Into Your Competitors' Every Move

Play Action:

Identify Your Top Competitors in a Specific Zip Code & See How Much Impression Share You Are Getting Compared to Your Competition.

Curious who you're actually competing against? Want to know what percentage of the marketplace you own compared to your competition? Of course you want this knowledge, any smart business owner would.

Auction insights is a useful report that allows you to compare your search performance with other advertisers. These are your competitors who are participating in the same auctions you are.

The report gives you valuable knowledge like:

- The total number of impressions you received divided by the total market search volume.

- Your average position compared to everyone else in your market.

- You overlap rate- which is a measurement of how often a competitor's ad receives an impression at the same rate as you.

- Outranking share- the number of times your ad ranked higher in the auction compared to a competitors.

The auction insights report is a helpful tool that will assist you in making decisions about how to manage your account. You'll see real opportunities to increase or decrease your bidding and budget. It shows you where you're succeeding and where you're missing opportunities.

Settings	Ads	Keywords	Audiences	Ad extensions	Dimensions	▼

←	Segment ▾	Filter ▾	Columns ▾	⬇

Auction insights report

See how you're performing compared to other advertisers. With the Auction insights report, you can see how successful your keywords, ad groups, or campaigns are in terms of impression share, average position and other statistics, in relation to those of other advertisers who are participating in the same auctions. Note: the information in this report is based on Google Search traffic for the date range you selected.

56% of available impressions (from 5 keywords) were used to generate this report. Learn more

Display url domain ⓘ	Impression share ⓘ ▲	Avg. position ⓘ	Overlap rate ⓘ	Position above rate ⓘ	Top of page rate ⓘ
You	80.46%	3	--	--	44.96%
▓▓▓▓.m	67.38%	2.8	73.81%	64.03%	60.47%
▓▓▓▓.com	48.86%	4.5	57.52%	28.62%	34.99%
▓▓▓▓s.com	47.44%	2.8	52.21%	57.97%	52.55%
▓▓▓▓tool.com	32.05%	1.8	35.93%	85.22%	84.44%
▓▓▓▓.com	30.46%	6.5	35.75%	3.96%	0.00%
▓▓▓▓so.com	20.37%	4.9	24.07%	29.41%	24.48%
▓▓▓▓.ym	15.24%	4.6	17.52%	38.36%	0.00%

fig. 9-1

Pulling this report at the adgroup level is the best option because it gives you a full break down of that particular campaign segment. An adgroup is simply one or more ads that share a similar target and the same campaign settings like geo-location.

Steve's PPC Breakdown

Track Competitors at a Hyper Local Level

Personally, I like to run my campaigns at the city level so I can get a complete breakdown of all the competitive insights in a given zip code. I have many clients who will cover a 25-mile radius or greater, so running a city campaign gives me the hyper-local reporting I need. I can view the strategy of local competitors at the zip code level- something you would not get if your campaign blanketed an entire region vs a single zip code.

I review this information weekly and save the historical reports so I can reference them. By doing this, I'm able to identify competitors who may run out of budget earlier in the month. I can also see competitors who try Google Ads and give up. By getting a feel for how often a competitor is pausing and running their ads and tracking movement, I'm able to make an educated guess as to whether my competitor's account is actually being managed or is on "set and forget" cruise control.

The auction insights reports is an extremely powerful tool when you are using it this way.

PPC Scorecard

You Have Set Up Your Campaigns at the Local City Level so You Can Track Competitor Movement by Zip Code Using Google's Auction Insights Report.

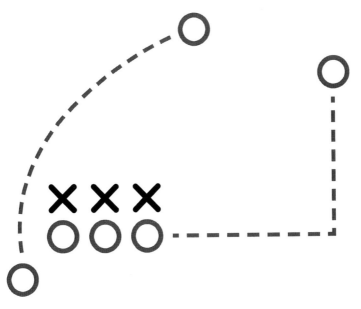

Play #9 / How To Get X-Ray Vision Into Your Competitor's Every Move

PLAY #10

7 Reasons Why Your Ads Aren't Showing and How To Fix Them

Play Action:

Identify and Take Action On Problem Keywords Not Triggering Your Ads.

Have you ever Googled one of your keywords only to be frustrated with the realization that your ads are not triggering?

There are several reasons why this might occur and luckily, none of them are too complicated to fix. Within your Google Ad account in the keyword section, you will find the keyword status column. Your keyword status is very important because it tells you if your ad is showing to your audience. See below for an example of what your status column looks like.

fig. 10-1: Status column within Google Ad

Let's explore some reasons why your ad may not be showing:

1. The keyword, adgroup, or campaign has been paused.

2. The keyword is under review. Google is evaluating your keyword and will approve or disapprove it.

3. Your keyword is below the first page bid estimate. This means you are not bidding enough on it to show on the first page of results.

4. The keyword has been disapproved. Google feels as though your keyword is not up to their standards or may be served a limited basis if they believe you are infringing upon a federally protected landmark or are in a grey area violating their terms of service.

5. The keyword is not eligible because there is very little search volume or it may not be relevant to people's searches. The keyword could also be too specific or unusual to show.

6. The keyword may be relevant but have a quality score that's too low. You'll want to make adjustments to your ads and landing pages in hopes of improving your quality score.

7. You may have a negative keyword that conflicts with the keyword you're attempting to drive traffic with. You can simply remove the negative keyword from your negative list.

By looking at these potential reasons and digging into the root of the problem, you can quickly assess what's happening with your ads. You can also run a keyword diagnostic report within the keyword section. This report will provide you a list of your entire keyword catalog along with their status as well as a reason why your ad is not showing.

Once you've solved your immediate keyword issues, you'll want to evaluate your keywords (and their statuses) on a monthly basis to see if any of them require your immediate attention.

PPC Scorecard

You Have Identified All Keywords Not Eligible to Run By Running a Keyword Diagnostic Report and Have a Plan to Fix Them.

PLAY

#11

How To Properly Set Your Budget So You Are Not Losing Sales Opportunities With Google's Keyword Planner.

Play Action:

Discover New Sales Opportunities and Drill into Your Local Market History to See How Much Search Volume Potential Exists. With this Information Develop an Ad Budget that Fits the Market Opportunity.

Have you heard about the Google keyword planner? You can use this Google provided tool to gain access to local market data right within your account. With the Google keyword planner you can see search volume, historical metrics for your keywords, and forecasts that predict how your keywords might perform in the future. This tool has come a long way since its inception with greater accuracy and improved metrics especially at a local level.

A great way to brainstorm new keywords is by entering your website (or the website of one of your competitors). The keyword planner will scan the site for relevant keywords and identify new opportunities for you to drive traffic and capture leads.

But how do you morph this information into a conversion plan? Once you establish your keyword portfolio you can plug it into the forecast engine. By breaking this plan down by zip code you'll be seeing the estimated number of searches in a given area. You can plug in your current conversion rate and the absolute highest amount you're willing to pay for a click. You'll even be able to see how much traffic you'll drive in.

Perhaps one of the best features of the keyword planner is that it lets you see historical market information. I'm sure you've heard the old saying, *"history repeats itself."* Looking back at past spend performance in your market is a skillful way to craft a budget that makes sense now.

You can also see how much opportunity exists in the market and what size budget makes sense for your area. All too often people set artificial budgets without really understanding the potential that's out there. Why not base your budget off something a little more concrete? This one tool gives you the data and confidence to make smarter budget decisions. See an example of the keyword planner below.

fig. 11-1: Keyword planner

Don't leave opportunity on the table. By understanding the ebb and flow of your market you'll be ready to seize the moments as they arise and make the most out of your ad spend.

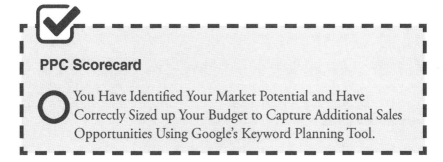

PPC Scorecard

You Have Identified Your Market Potential and Have Correctly Sized up Your Budget to Capture Additional Sales Opportunities Using Google's Keyword Planning Tool.

PLAY #12
Grow Sales in Your Backyard With Location-Based Mobile Search

Play Action:

Get in the Location Based Mobile Search Game and Build City Specific Campaigns to Attract Prospects Looking to do Business with a Local Professional.

People like to buy from people who they know, like, and trust. They want to feel like they're buying from the business down the street, even if your shop is a town or two away. It should come as no surprise that there is evidence of a growing increase in local city based and location-based searches.

More than 50% of the traffic I generate for my clients will result in terms that include phrases that involve the city name along with the type of service or product. For instance, *"Denver Dentist,"* or *"Sacramento Plumber,"* or *"Boston Heating Contractor"* along with terms that involve the phrase "near me" like *"Electrician Near Me,"* as an example.

What is really interesting is that close to 70% of these local searches come in by way of a **mobile device**. When you know this information you can really change the game on how you manage your ad campaigns.

One smart tactic to capitalize on this trend is to organize your campaigns and break them down by individual city or zip code, treating each city as if it were the only one you serviced. Why do this? What results can you expect to see?

Breaking campaigns down at the city level allows you to:

○ Inject the name of the city in your ad copy which makes you appear hyper-local to potential customers. When you do this you'll notice your response or click through rate increases exponentially.

○ Create very specific landing pages to support each one of these campaigns. This will help increase your lead conversion rate. You'll generate more leads and decrease your overall cost to acquire new clients.

The fact is, most people are searching at a local level when it comes to hiring a service professional or purchasing a product that requires an installation. When you have this knowledge and utilize this feedback in your campaigns, you can start to truly dial in your budget and apply it to both the campaigns and devices that deliver the most qualified traffic.

 Steve's PPC Breakdown

If you are just starting out or you want to gradually grow with Google Ads, the best place to start is to launch local city campaigns for the products and services you offer. Create an experience where your buyers see the name of the city or town where they live or work. This will give you the confidence you need to scale your campaigns because if done correctly, you'll start to generate leads. Once you see qualified lead activity come through your pipeline you can stack on additional campaigns to increase volume.

With Google, the power is in your hands. Control where your ads appear with city-based or radius based targeting. Control how your ads appear to your audience by understanding what they're looking for. Focus your budget on the devices where the qualified traffic is searching. Most importantly, control the experience your prospect enters into via your landing pages.

PPC Scorecard

You Have Implemented Location-Based Search Campaigns Focused on Mobile Devices to Attract Buyers Wanting to do Business with a Local Professional.

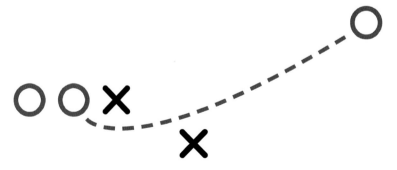

Play #12 / Grow Sales in Your Backyard With Location Based Mobile

PLAY #13 | Are You Taking Advantage of Voice Search?

Play Action:

Get Ahead of the Curve and Setup a Voice Search Campaign to Target Prospects Who Use Voice Assistants.

"Ok Google, tell me about voice search."

One in five mobile searches are made by voice search versus typing into a search bar. As more and more people are having conversations with Siri, Google Assistant, Windows Cortana, Alexa and other voice assistants, it's vital that your campaigns are optimized for voice search.

People are using their assistants because:

O   They're fun to use.

X   They're considered cool in this age of tech.

X   They're delivering faster results than firing up an app and typing.

O   They're useful when hands are full or when vision is occupied i.e. driving.

This means if it hasn't happened already ads are coming to voice search. In fact, as this article is being written Google is starting to test ads on Google Assistant. You want to anticipate conversational searches as more and more assistants monetize their service with advertising. You can do this by optimizing campaigns with natural language which include both questions and commands along with consideration to time and place.

Examples:

O   Who is the best air conditioner contractor in the city?

X   Find me an air conditioner contractor.

X   Find me the closest air conditioner contractor.

O   Find me an air conditioner contractor who is open now.

X   Find me an air conditioner contractor in Boston, MA.

O   Is there an air conditioner contractor open now?

Designing your campaigns to fit the way your prospects will be receiving them is one of the best ways you can stay ahead of the curve and get in front of these search opportunities.

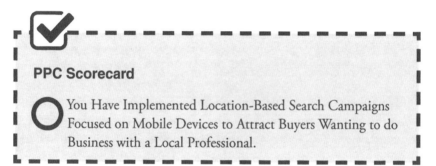

PPC Scorecard

O   You Have Implemented Location-Based Search Campaigns Focused on Mobile Devices to Attract Buyers Wanting to do Business with a Local Professional.

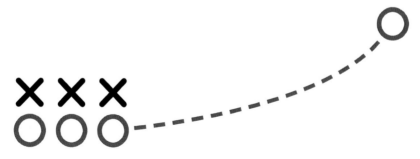

Play #13 / Are You Taking Advantage of Voice Search?

PLAY #14

Discover a Keyword Magic Trick That Will Save You a Ton of Time

Play Action:

Use Google's Keyword Insertion Tool to Create Unique Ads For Every Keyword.

Using keyword insertion can help you save time scaling campaigns, improve response, and increase conversion rates.

It's always a best practice to include your keywords in your ad copy and on your landing pages. You can do this manually by building ads from scratch for every single keyword or (if you like working smarter) you can take advantage of Google's keyword insertion feature.

Keyword insertion lets you automatically update your ads with the keywords in your Google campaign. This means that when someone types in the term you're bidding on the keyword will automatically show in your ad copy. This helps you save a lot of time. It will also help your ads appear to be more relevant to users searching for your products and services.

Steve's PPC Breakdown

Let's explore how keyword insertion actually works. Essentially, you plug this special piece of code {KeyWord: enterkeyword} right into your ads. When a searcher uses one of your keywords in their search, Google Ads will automatically replace the code with the keyword that triggered your ads.

Steve's PPC Breakdown *(continued)*

In addition, if you have a savvy developer who understands code you can carry the keyword right over to your landing pages. This will help you save a lot of time duplicating pages for specific keywords, ultimately improving your conversion rates and overall quality score.

Now, I'm personally not a big fan of automated keyword insertion. I like to manually create hand-crafted ads for my clients. However, if you aren't creating customized ads for each keyword today then this tool would act as a great first step in creating a unified and consistent experience for each interested prospect looking for your products and services. You can essentially use this tool up front to save time and see which keywords are getting the bulk of the traffic and focus your energy by creating custom ads for the keywords that count.

Keyword insertion is an advanced Google Ads tool that comes in handy when you are running a large scale campaign and you want to work smarter, not harder in creating a lot of customized ads for your audience.

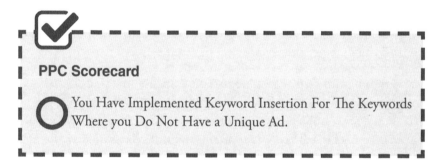

PPC Scorecard

You Have Implemented Keyword Insertion For The Keywords Where you Do Not Have a Unique Ad.

PLAY #15 | **Improve Keyword Performance with Google Recommendations**

Play Action:

Use Google's Recommendation Dashboard to Implement Suggested Improvements Offered By Google Artificial Intelligence.

In the past, discovering new search terms and making improvements to your keyword portfolio had to be done manually using the Search Terms Report. Now, Google's Recommendations Dashboard gives you a visual representation of the search terms report that does a lot of the work for you by offering you strategic recommendations based on the activity of your campaigns.

Within the Keyword Recommendations Dashboard Google will offer you one of the many following suggestions based on Google AI:

- How to reach additional customers and drive additional traffic in other areas.

- Providing you with visibility into overlapping or redundant keywords.

- Areas where you can add audience reporting. You'll be able to see how certain demographic segments are performing in your market.

- How you can personalize ads to your existing customers.

- The identification of keywords that are not serving an ad.

○   Areas where you can serve dynamic ads in an effort to capture relevant business you may be missing.

✗   And most important, new keyword opportunities you can add to capture additional revenue opportunities.

fig. 15-1: Google recommendations

This is just one section of Google's recommendation section. There are other opportunities within this dashboard where Google is acting as your "coach," providing you with action items you can implement to help you get a better result. You get an optimization grade of percentage complete, with 100% as your optimal score.

The recommendations are essentially a checklist of items you can follow to get incremental improvements in your performance. I recommend going through them on a monthly basis and implementing or dismissing the recommendations that make sense to your strategy.

But be careful about accepting all of Google's recommendations. They are not perfect. They are done by a machine, not a human. If you accept a recommendation they will automatically make the adjustments to your given campaigns. Accepting all recommendations can easily disrupt your account if you are unsure about the recommendation outcome.

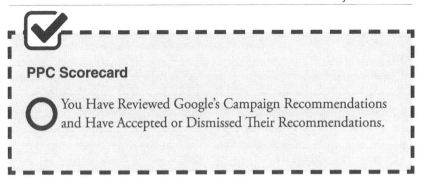

PPC Scorecard

You Have Reviewed Google's Campaign Recommendations and Have Accepted or Dismissed Their Recommendations.

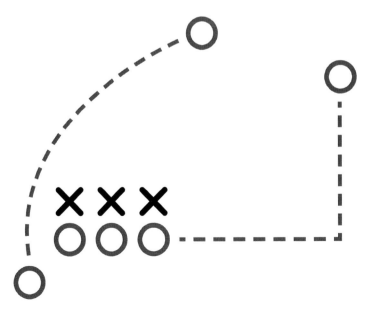

Play #15 / Improve Keyword Performance with Google Recommendations

"It's not whether you get knocked down; it's whether you get up."

-Vince Lombardi

WELCOME TO THE ONLINE ADVERTISING GAME

Are You Ready To Attend Google Ads Training Camp?

Do you want to craft the best ad copy possible so you can compete and win in your local market but don't know where to begin? In the upcoming sections I'm going to give you an inside look into my proven "Google Ad Blueprint."

I'm going to start by walking you through step-by-step, the basic foundations of writing effective ad copy for Google Ads that will help you win more business. Next, I'll take you behind the scenes and explain to you the different types of Google ad formats and how to best use them. You'll see what works and what doesn't. And finally, I'm going to show you how you can use Google's ad extensions to make your ads work harder.

Below you'll find an outline of everything we're going to tackle together along with questions you should ask yourself to get prepared for the road ahead. Get ready to increase response rates, improve lead quality and get the most you can out of Google's advertising features.

In The Proven Ad Copy Formula Section You'll Discover:

○ How to write ads that speak to the intentions of the buyer.

✗ The philosophies I've learned in my career as it relates to developing a killer offer.

○ And all of the critical components that go into a winning ad.

Next, we'll discuss how Google makes it easy to customize your ads with more options than ever before. You'll take a lot of factors into consideration when deciding what features to take advantage of, but ultimately it's all about tailoring your ads to your prospect's intent.

In The Google Ad Blueprint Section You'll Learn:

✗ All of the different types of Google ad campaigns you can implement and how they might fit into your goals.

○ How to master click-through-rate performance improvement. After completing the scorecard checks in this section you'll start to see your click-through rates improve while at the same time helping you enhance lead quality and decrease your overall cost per click.

○   How to use Google's ad tools to test your messaging and determine what works best.

○   Plus, you'll see how much real estate you can really own once you understand and implement Google's new expanded text ads.

And finally, advertising on Google has come a long way. In the past, you were once limited to two headlines and one description line with less characters. Now you have more opportunity than ever to attract and provide details to the prospects you want to do business with by taking advantage of Google's Ad Extensions.

In this section I'm going to walk you through the most relevant Google Ad Extensions related to lead generation.

In The Google Ad Extensions Section You'll See:

✗   How you can add additional sales copy to your core ad and say what you couldn't say in your headlines.

✗   How you can highlight sales, deals and special offers, build trust, and show off your reviews.

○   How you can drive in more phone calls.

✗   How you can add additional height on your ads.

○   How you can strategically use certain ad extensions by taking advantage of custom scheduling.

○   Plus, if you advertise on TV, radio, or print I'll show you how to protect your brand and drive engagement with this audience.

There's more options than ever before when it comes to building and customizing your ads. If you've been using the same ad formats with limited success, this section will help you explore Google's newest options and use them to win business. Now that I've outlined our game plan, let's get to work on crafting a Google ad that helps you improve response rates, lowers lead cost, and help you get the most out of your pay-per-click campaigns.

"It's hard to beat a person who never gives up."

-Babe Ruth

SECTION #2 THE PROVEN AD COPY FORMULA

WIN MORE BUSINESS WITH AN ADVERTISEMENT THAT WORKS.

You'll Learn How To Create an Irresistible Offer That Will Help You Increase Sales, Make it Easier For Buyers to Purchase From You, Speed Up Your Sales Cycles and Set Your Business Apart From Your Competition.

Kill The Competition: 7 Rules In Creating a Compelling Offer to Attract Your Best Customers

Play Action:

Consider Obstacles in Your Sales Process Holding You Back Today and Make Adjustments to Accelerate Revenue Production.

One aspect I love about my job is that I get to write a lot of ads for a living. Unlike radio, TV or print, I can pretty much enjoy the fruit of my labor in less than an hour by seeing results with Google Ads. That's how fast I can tell whether my ad appeals to a buyer or not. That's the beauty of Google Ads. You can tell if you have a winner or a dud right away and you can make the necessary adjustments to fine tune your message.

I put in a lot of thought when I develop ad copy for my clients. In fact, before I write a Google Ad I like to create a sales letter and brainstorm all of the components that go into an ad. I follow a checklist and process I developed called **The Ad Copy Formula** which makes it pretty easy to get a hand-crafted ad out the door. I'm going to outline my formula in this section.

I sit down and think about all of the factors that go into the psychology of the sale. The goal of an ad is to create interest and have your prospect take action. The ad directs them to the first step in your sales process. There are some basic philosophies I want to share with you before getting into the Ad Copy Formula. I suppose you can call these rules, but really they are the fundamentals in ad copy strategy.

I didn't make these up and I'm not here to sell you on them as my own. Over the years I have intensely studied copywriters like Gary Halbert, Dan Kennedy and John Carlton. My wife gives me a hard time when I pick apart billboards or criticize local companies who buy full page color ads in local magazines without putting in a phone number!

I have always been a lifelong student in the art of advertising. A lot I've learned through trial and error myself. I'm a big fan of the AMC series Mad Men, and I enjoy the history of ads. From studying PT Barnum and how he was able to leverage advertising to sell out crowds for his Barnum & Bailey Circus to how Sears used advertising to sell complete homes in a magazine that arrived by train for homeowners to construct just like you would if you purchased something from Ikea. I eat this stuff up and get really excited about it.

Let me fill you in on a fun fact: The first newspaper advertisement was published in 1704 in the Boston News-Letter. It was an announcement seeking a buyer for an Oyster Bay, Long Island estate. Here's a copy of the ad:

fig. 16-1: First newspaper advertisement

And so it began, advertising in colonial America. Not much has changed since that time. Dan Kennedy, in his book Magnetic Marketing discusses market, message and media. In short, as long as you have a market and the right message you just plug those elements into the media.

In the first ever newspaper ad, the seller knows the market of new settlers looking for land, uses a message that highlights the amenities of the land, and plugs it into the media of the time- the local newspaper.

Online marketing is just another media outlet where you can make an investment in advertising. The same message that's working for you on Google Ads will also work for you in print, on TV and on the radio. Most advertising campaigns fail because one or more of the components of the market, message or media was wrong or completely missing.

Play #16 / Kill The Competition: 7 Rules In Creating a Compelling Offer

So without getting too deep into the weeds, because I can discuss this topic until I'm blue in the face, I'm going to outline the philosophies I've learned throughout the years. All of the essential rules that go into creating a killer offer so someone will ultimately get interested and enter your sales process to buy from you.

Here they are:

1. Make it easy for prospects to say yes.

- O   Eliminate any obstacles to doing business with you.
- ✕   Identify areas now where you might be losing opportunities.
- O   If buyers are conditioned to purchase a certain way do not reinvent the wheel.

I work with a lot of home service companies that sell water heater replacement services. If you think about water heaters, the first thing that comes to mind is probably Home Depot, Lowes, Sears, Menards, or another big box store. There's a good chance you have a credit card to one of these stores with some incentive to buy from them. These companies make it easy for you to call an 800 number and receive instant installed water heater pricing right over the phone. They'll send a plumber out the same day to replace your water heater.

All too often in this situation, a lot of local home service companies who want this business don't do that. They want to go out and perform an inspection, evaluate the scope of work and over complicate a simple water heater replacement. Your current sales process can be creating barriers to entry and ultimately be costing you real revenue opportunities. When you restrict your sales process you also restrict your ability to compete in your advertising. My best performing water heater ad includes the phrase *"Call Now For Instant Over The Phone Pricing."*

When working with my clients who install or replace water heaters I coach them to give pricing over the phone. The buyers purchasing this specific product want it today and are conditioned by the big box stores to buy online or over the phone without jumping through many hoops. People don't have time for long, drawn out sales processes. You can easily increase sales by eliminating barriers and restrictions. Go ahead and open things up. You'll see how you can streamline sales opportunities and increase your revenue with a few adjustments.

2. Next, make the offer something that cannot be refused. Make it irresistible, bold, too good to be true. Something your competitors are not doing.

Here are some great examples of campaigns I'm currently running with high response rates:

- O   A drain cleaning company advertising $99 cleaning specials.

- X   Heating and cooling companies who advertise a free furnace with any ac replacement.

- O   A carpet cleaning company who advertises, "Buy 2 rooms get the 3rd free!"

- X   A local eye doctor who sells eyeglasses, "Buy one pair, get the 2nd pair half off."

- O   An orthodontist selling Invisalign, "A Smile You'll Love for Only $49/mo."

3. Build your marketing strategy around the offer.

What's your endgame?

- X   If you are in the business of long term client relationships, spending a little money now to make a lot of money over time could be the right move. It might be a good strategy to develop a loss leader. A loss-leader is something you can offer to get your foot in the door and offer a service at a loss (or break even) in an effort to capture the customer and grow revenue through the lifetime value of the relationship.

- O   If you offer a one time purchase at a higher transaction value, your endgame may be maximizing the one-time sale and capturing a referral through offering a great experience.

4. Give your offer a name

○ Offers always sound better when there's a name attached or it's presented as a package. When you go to McDonalds you don't order a Big Mac, fries, and a coke. You order an Extra Value Meal which includes all of those things. Make it appealing to receive multiple services under one great offer. Combine elements of your product or service delivery and create a lot of value.

5. Incentives/Coupon Discounting

○ I'm not a big fan of discounting or offering coupons to get business, but they do work especially if you want to drive volume in a transactional sale that's easy to deliver.

6. Distinct/Unique

○ Make sure your offer is unique enough that no one else is doing the same thing and, if they tried to replicate what you're doing, they'd have operational challenges attempting to implement it.

7. Sell the benefits not the service. Focus on the outcome

✗ People buy the carpet cleaning because they want fresh, clean carpets to breathe easier and eliminate smells. They can care less about scotch guard.

○ People buy home additions to their home to increase the value of their home or to enjoy a larger living space. They don't want to know what kind of drywall is being used.

✗ People buy water heaters because they want hot showers and clean dishes. Most people won't worry about which heating element was used in the tank.

Always lead with the benefits and the emotional outcome the buyer will receive. People are looking to satisfy a need or want, so tell them how you'll solve that problem.

Don't put your ads out there for the world to see incomplete. Brush up on these key components and get to work creating your own killer offer!

PPC Scorecard

Adjust Your Ads So They Do Not Restrict Your Sales Goals. Create Compelling Messages that Include Benefits, Are Unique in Your Market, Include an Irresistible Offer and Make it Easy for Buyers to Take the Next Step in Your Sales Process.

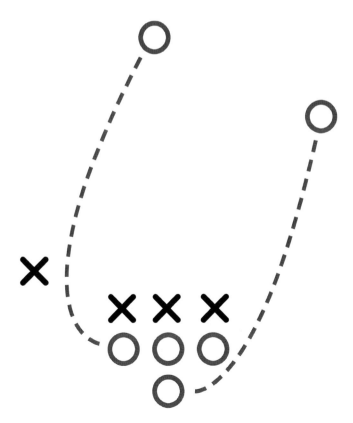

Play #16 / Kill The Competition: 7 Rules In Creating a Compelling Offer

PLAY #17

How To Generate Consistent Sales with a Strong Call-to-Action

Play Action:

Create and Implement a Call-To-Action in Your Ad Copy.

The first part of the Proven Ad Copy Formula is the Call-to-Action Factor. A great call to action or CTA clearly tells the buyer what to do next if they're interested in moving forward in your sales process.

A good call to action uses an instructive command. Try some of these out for size:

- ○ "Call now"
- ✕ "Fill out this form"
- ○ "Buy now"

A good call to action will include your offer and/or a component of speed:

- ○ "Call now for same day service"
- ✕ "Call now for a free in-home estimate"

Use instant gratification in your call to action:

- ○ "Call now to speak to a live operator"
- ✕ "Call now and get instant pricing"
- ○ "Fill out this form for an immediate call back"

Know your devices and your sales process to determine which one to use. "Call now" is going to be a better CTA for mobile devices, while a form fill is more likely on a desktop for a high ticket, longer sales cycle purchase.

Stay clear of complicating your call to action and don't have more than one. Often times people try to do too much, which can confuse the goal for your prospect and leave them doing the wrong thing or worse- nothing at all. Eliminate confusing options by keeping it simple.

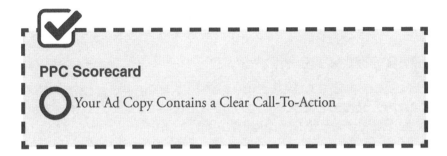

PPC Scorecard

◯ Your Ad Copy Contains a Clear Call-To-Action

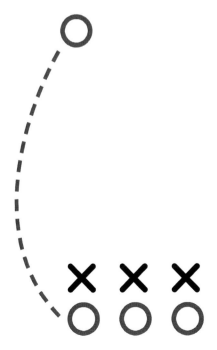

Play #17 / How To Generate Consistent Sales with a Strong Call-to-Action

How To Use Speed in Your Sales Process to Eliminate Price Objections

Play Action:

Develop a Speed Component in Your Ad Copy to Target Buyers Looking to Purchase Your Products and Services Right Now

How fast can you solve a prospect's problem, challenge, or goal?

Speed sells. When the threshold for pain is at its highest, or if you're dealing with a buyer who wants instant gratification or convenience the more likely speed is going to be the priority and price is not going to be a concern.

Amazon does a great job of doing this. With its acquisition of Whole Foods, Amazon is turning the supermarket into a delivery company. The perception of being the high-priced organic supermarket is quickly being replaced by the image of the supermarket that delivers convenience-groceries delivered within 2 hours.

By implementing a speed component to their business model, Whole Foods can still charge a premium for its products through their app Prime Now. Instead of going to the grocery store and battling through the aisles just to wait in congested lines, I can easily fill up my shopping cart on my smartphone while watching the morning news. By dinner time all of my groceries will have been delivered. This saves me a lot of time that I can spend doing the things I enjoy.

This is a great example of delivering speed. Where are the opportunities in your business where you can deliver on speed and attract the "give-it-to-me-now" buyer?

Here are some examples:

○ A dentist offering flexible weekend appointments so patients don't miss work.

✗ A kitchen and bathroom remodeling company that delivers samples on wheels so people don't have to go to a showroom and can shop from their own home.

○ An air conditioner contractor who will respond within 60-minutes when your air conditioner breaks down on a 90 degree humid day.

○ A heating contractor who offers next day replacement on heating equipment when your furnace fails during a record cold snap.

○ An auto repair mechanic who can deliver oil changes in 20 minutes or less.

Always remember what you're selling and who you're advertising it to. This will help you plan accordingly and use speed to your advantage.

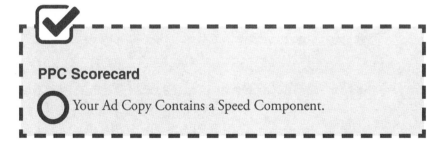

PPC Scorecard

○ Your Ad Copy Contains a Speed Component.

How To Set Your Business Apart From The Competition by Adding Tremendous Value To Your Offers

Play Action:

Develop a Value Component and Work it in to Your Core Offer to Differentiate Your Business From Your Competition.

Put yourself in the buyer's shoes. Let's assume there is another company in your market with a similar experience, similar reviews, and a similar price point. When all things are equal it's hard to make a buying decision, especially when there's more than one good choice.

The value factor is the one thing that will help push your company over the edge in being the one the buyer selects. Value is the icing on the cake. It's the one thing you can do to sweeten the deal and make the sale.

Value is something extra the buyer gets so they feel like they're getting more when comparatively things feel the same. It makes the buyer feel special, like they are getting a deal. Although it may not seem like something big to you, it could be the difference between making the sale or losing the potential customer. There's a very good chance you are already delivering the value component in your service or product delivery, but you're just not marketing it. You include it without positioning it as an "extra" to customers.

Here's some examples of building value in your offer:

○ If you sell eyeglasses for instance, throw in free eyeglass cleaner or offer free adjustments for 3 years. I have a three-year-old son who loves to take my glasses and bends them. My local eyeglass shop knows me by first name and fixes them for me without charging me.

○ If you install air conditioners, throw in free filters for the first year.

○ If you replace tires, throw in a free oil change.

✗ If you are an auto dealer include a lifetime of free oil changes.

○ If you're a landscaper who sells mulch include a lawn service for free.

You get the point. These are all examples of adding value to an offer. If you watch infomercials you'll see value being built at every step of the way. Offers that *double the quantity for free*, or *buy 2 get 1 free*. Or if you place an order, you might get a complimentary product included with the purchase.

What is something that you normally offer anyway in a sale that you can separate from your core offer? You probably have something in mind at this point. Add it in as a bonus to create tremendous value in your offer.

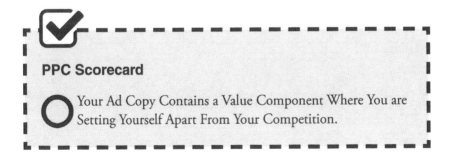

PPC Scorecard

○ Your Ad Copy Contains a Value Component Where You are Setting Yourself Apart From Your Competition.

PLAY #20

How To Generate More Leads By Giving Buyers What They Really Want

Play Action:

Develop and Implement a List of Benefits that Align With Your Product and Service Offerings to Attract Buyers Who Shop on Emotion.

"What's in it for me?" The one important question your ads need to answer.

What are the primary benefits of the product and/or services you're offering? How is purchasing from you going to impact my life or solve my challenge or goal? In order to effectively advertise to your prospects, you'll first need to think like them by appealing to the emotional impact your product or service delivers.

Here are some examples:

- If you are an Opthamoligist selling laser eye surgery, you're selling the beautiful experiences your clients will be able to enjoy with clarity of sight.

- If you replace windows you're selling lower utility costs, warmth and comfort, or you're preventing an old window from falling on a child.

- If you sell fishing charters you're selling relaxation and the spirit of adventure.

These are just examples of what a benefit might sound like. A good benefit will always trigger an emotional response from the buyer.

I recently purchased new carbon monoxide detectors for my home because I want to keep my family safe. I didn't buy them because the carbon monoxide detectors had a digital readout, an 85db alarm, and included a battery backup. These things are important but they are features, not benefits.

What are the primary benefits of your product or service offering? Are you listing them in your ads? By tapping into this emotional response you can create a higher response rate from potential customers.

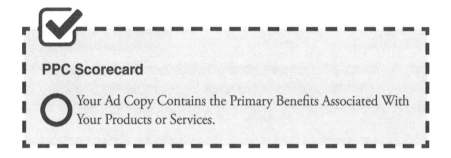

PPC Scorecard

Your Ad Copy Contains the Primary Benefits Associated With Your Products or Services.

PLAY #21 — **How To Write a Bold Guarantee That Will Help You Win More Business**

Play Action:

Create and Implement a Bullet Proof Promise in Your Ad Copy to Put Prospects at Ease in Doing Business With You.

What is your promise to your client? What are you willing to guarantee them long after you deliver your product or service?

When it comes to creating your promise, the bolder the better. Be sure to make it very descriptive, too. Tell your future customers exactly what you're offering and keep it in alignment with your product and/or services.

A great promise also includes risk reversal. This is how you ease the buyer's greatest concern by taking away any risks they might feel they have. Of course, this means you have to take action once the buyer's assumed risk happens. It's easier to move a sale forward once you reduce the risk or eliminate it altogether. Get rid of the hurdles for your prospective customer and sweeten the promise by adding something extra to it.

Here's a <u>bad example</u> of a promise:

"100% satisfaction guaranteed." This is a "so what?" kind of promise. It's overdone, it's broad and it's not good enough. Anyone can say this. You want a promise that you can live up to, but it has to be something your competition can't replicate. That's why it must be bold and unique.

Here's a good example of a promise:

"10 year bumper to bumper 100,000 mile no breakdown guarantee. If your new vehicle breaks down, we'll fix it free and give you a rental." This is a great example of a promise a car dealership might make. Notice how specific it is. It speaks to the largest concerns a potential customer might have in that situation.

Steve's PPC Breakdown:

Here's a great format for a risk reversal that anyone can use.

If for any reason whatsoever {enter buyer's assumed risk}, we will {promise/action}. Plus we'll {how you'll make it right} by {addition promise.}

Let's look at an example of this in action:

"If for any reason {your new central air conditioner breaks down within the first 10 years of installation} we will {fix it or replace it for free.} Plus, we'll {make it certain you'll always be comfortable}, even if we have to {put you and your family in a hotel room for a night.}

The promise allows the customer to stop worrying about the negatives that could happen by giving them added security. From here they'll feel comfortable with the sale knowing you stand behind your product or service.

PPC Scorecard

 Your Ad Copy Contains Risk Reversal and Clearly States a Bold Promise or Guarantee.

PLAY #22 | People Buy From People They Know, Like and *Trust*

Play Action:

Identify Trust Signals in Your Business and Communicate Them in Your Ad Copy.

We live in a day and age where your reputation is public knowledge. Luckily, you can use this to your advantage. Gathering positive reviews and testimonials in places like Google, Facebook, and Yelp can really help you make additional sales.

There's no better form of advertising than somebody else's positive affirmation and praise towards their experience working with your company. It gives you the ability to say, *"Don't take my word for it. Here's what my customers are saying…"*

There are many ways to build trust in your ads. The best way is to put a number of positive reviews right in the ad copy.

For example:

- ○ "Over 500 5-Star Reviews On Google." This is something customers can go verify, but will most likely take at face value and convince them to click on your ad.

- ○ You can also set up Google's Seller Ratings which will pull your Google reviews automatically and associate them to your ads. If you've ever seen a Google Ad that had stars attached to them, this is what it is. I have a whole chapter dedicated to Google Seller Ratings up ahead.

Another way to build trust is to affiliate your brand with a well-known trusted entity like the BBB. You can say "A+ BBB Rating" in your ad copy when you are an accredited member of the BBB who pays their dues.

Even your years in business can be a trust factor because it points to your experience, i.e. "Trusted Since 1973." You want prospects to feel that they can count on your company to get the job done, even before they've spoken with you.

Always remember that people are strongly influenced by reviews. A good majority are doing their homework before they call you. Positive reviews will help you increase your response and conversion rates. They will make your core offer that much more powerful.

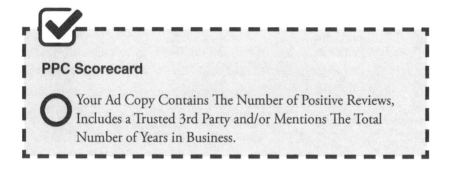

PPC Scorecard

O Your Ad Copy Contains The Number of Positive Reviews, Includes a Trusted 3rd Party and/or Mentions The Total Number of Years in Business.

How To Target the 8 out of 10 Buyers Who Shop Local

Play Action:

Work The City Name and a Local Phone Line into Your Ad Copy to Get in Front of Local Buyers.

I'm the type of guy who likes to hire and buy local. I stay away from large multinational businesses as much as I can. I like to support local business, and it turns out I'm not alone.

According to a recent survey conducted by The Local Search Association, 8 out of 10 Americans use local businesses. And this number is expected to continue to increase with time. Consumers believe that a local business will provide service that's better quality, more personalized, and more reliable.

That's why it's important to give potential buyer's the appearance you are the local choice. Your headquarters may not be in the same city as the prospect, but there's a good chance you have an employee or two from that area. Unfortunately, you can't be in every customer's neighborhood, but you can keep it local in your ad copy and landing pages.

Here are a couple ways to bring in local aspects to your ads:

○   Incorporate the name of the city you're targeting in your ad copy. An example here is: "Serving the Local Fort Worth Community Since 1973!". Let them know you've worked in their neighborhood before, and can be there again to help them.

O   Use a local phone number vs an 800 number for your phone lines. People want to see their area code on the landing page so they know you are close by. An 800 number is too generic and distances you from the customer. In my experience, a local phone line has always outperformed an 800 number when it comes to targeting a local audience.

Being local implies trust, speed, and convenience. Make sure your prospects know you're the reliable go-to company in their local area. This one quick adjustment can boost your response rates right away.

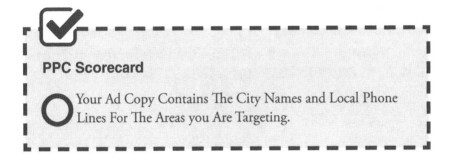

PPC Scorecard

Your Ad Copy Contains The City Names and Local Phone Lines For The Areas you Are Targeting.

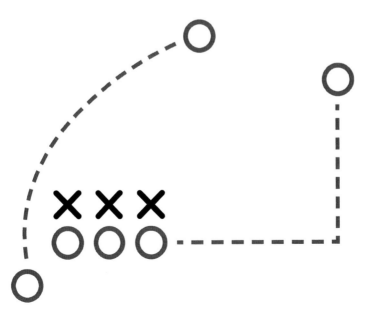

Play #23 / How To Target the 8 out of 10 Buyers Who Shop Local

PLAY #24 — 12 Ways You are Losing Sales and How To Fix It

Play Action:

Identify and Eliminate All of The Obstacles in Your Way Preventing You From Making Sales.

Are there obstacles preventing you from making the sale? Do your prospects have to jump through hoops in order to get to the next stage in your sales process? I have listened to thousands of calls over the years and am going to share with you some tips to eliminate barriers to entry by making things simple and easy for you to generate more business.

Some common barriers to entry:

1. Not answering the phone.

2. Allowing phone leads to be handled by a third party answering service. You lose control of the sales process this way. Most answering services cannot satisfy the buyers looking for instant gratification and often mishandle sales opportunities.

3. Sending hot prospects to *voicemail.* You'll find most people, especially if your ad is in the top position, will hang up once a voicemail prompt starts to play. They are already moving on to your competition. Live answer is always best.

4. Technical issues with your phone lines. Make sure you have enough lines available in your phone system to handle peak call volume throughout the day.

5. Charging upfront fees when your competition does not. I once worked with an air conditioning contractor who charged a callout fee to provide homeowners with a quote to replace their air conditioners. Most of his competitors were providing free in-home estimates, which is a very common practice in the industry. Needless to say, he didn't sell many air conditioner replacements.

6. Not accepting credit cards.

7. Not offering financing.

8. Not offering flexible appointments.

9. Not being open on the weekends or after hours if your ads run at these times.

10. Not following up in a timely fashion. The most common situation I see here is when you receive a form submission from a prospect requesting information about your solutions and the form sits in an email box. The longer it sits the lower the probability you'll have in closing a sale.

11. Confusion in your sales process. Trying to diagnose a problem over the phone or fixing a problem without a proper consultation. If you answer your own phone right now- don't do it. You know way more than everybody else and you might end up talking yourself out of a sale. Get somebody else to qualify opportunities. If you walk into a doctor's office there's always a nurse or medical assistant who takes your blood pressure, gets your weight and handles all of the upfront data collection.

12. Over Complicating Things. Your offers should be real simple, cut and dry. Don't try to do too much. If it takes more than 30 seconds to explain and there's some sort of math equation to do business with you, people will not engage because you'll make their brains hurt. I see this a lot when there are multiple offers in a single ad for the same thing. When it comes to Google Ads, **the goal of the ad is to get the prospect to take the initial step in your sales process**, not close the sale. The closing requires human interaction.

Make it easy for people to do business with you. Write out your sales process so your prospects can see and understand exactly what it's going to be like for them, no surprises. Turn it into a pleasurable experience by eliminating barriers and making the process smooth and easy.

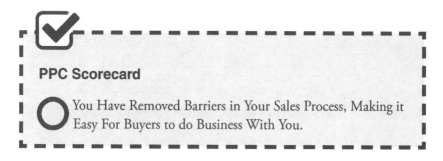

PPC Scorecard

O You Have Removed Barriers in Your Sales Process, Making it Easy For Buyers to do Business With You.

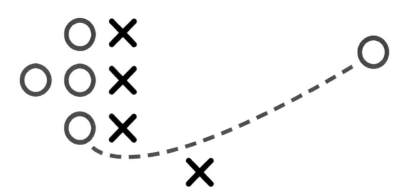

PLAY #25 | 10 Ways To Separate Your Business From the Competition

Play Action:

Identify Areas Where You Are Different in Your Local Market to Get an Edge Over Your Competition.

It's really easy for competitors to copy you. You know what they say, **imitation** is the sincerest form of **flattery**. To imitate someone is to pay the person a genuine compliment. Often an unintended one in the sales cycle. If you are losing opportunities to a competitor, it might be time to take a hard look at how different you are compared to them.

That's why if a competitor is apples to apples to you in sales, you've got to produce an orange. This is where differentiation comes in. What separates you from the pack?

Here are some ideas to help you express why your company is top choice quality:

1. Unique licensing you may hold.

2. Specialized training, education, and/or ongoing training.

3. Types of insurance you have to offer protection.

4. Years in business which indirectly sells your experience.

5. Financial stability. I work with a client who brings a letter with him from the bank on every sales call. He uses it to communicate to prospects that he has deep pockets and he'll finish the job.

6. Association with a trusted brand, group, or entity.

7. Special awards.

8. A specialized process, patents, trademarks etc.

9. Specific community involvement.

10. Case studies, reviews, testimonials. This builds trust, but also if you have an incredible amount this also differentiates you. i.e "The only company with more than 1,000 reviews!"

Remember that your prospects are choosing from a very large pool of candidates for the services and products they need. After doing a ton of research they may start to feel that the companies (you and your competitors) are starting to blend into one. Display what makes your company unique to win more business.

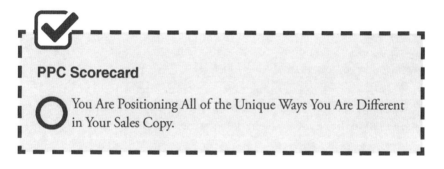

PPC Scorecard

You Are Positioning All of the Unique Ways You Are Different in Your Sales Copy.

How To Properly Use a Deadline to Accelerate Sales

Play Action:

Develop Urgency in Your Sales Process and Get Deals Done Faster by Implementing a Creative Deadline.

Deadlines push prospects to take action on a given date or during a specific event.

The auto industry is notorious for using deadlines. It seems like every major holiday there's a new special offer to purchase a vehicle. You can look to your local auto dealer for great examples in using a deadline to drive sales.

A deadline, when used correctly, creates urgency. When used improperly it just looks cheesy like an empty offer. You need to have a really good reason or story for why it exists and it has to be as genuine as possible. People can see right through artificial deadlines or deadlines put in place just for the hell of it.

Good deadline examples:

○ Limited time inventory special that ends on 10/31 because you offer a seasonal item and you have a surplus you need to clear out to make room for new products. You see auto dealerships discount current year vehicles to make room for new ones towards the end of each year. They have a legitimate reason.

○ Using scarcity or limited supply. "Only 2 appointments left today" or "Only 3 products left at this price." There's some exclusivity to this as well. It makes people feel like they've won something if they are just one of 2 people to get that appointment.

✗ Amazon does a good job creating urgency by stating that there are only {X amount} left in stock of a product then adding,"Want it tomorrow?"

fig. 26-1: Creating urgency in your ads

○ Use fear of missing out to your advantage as well. An example of this is:

> "One time neighborhood sales event, expires after we sell the first 10 units." You see a lot of these types of sales on Black Friday. Walmart sells a 70" flat screen TV for $400 when they are normally $999. "Once they're gone they're gone. Our sale ends at 11am." Use time sensitive offers to make your product or service seem like something they need to act on right now to get the best deal.

The classic end of the month sale isn't going to push the needle for you. It's been done time and time again. Deadlines exist everywhere. Create one with a solid reason and you'll increase sales.

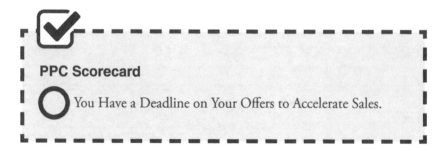

PPC Scorecard

○ You Have a Deadline on Your Offers to Accelerate Sales.

"You miss 100% of the shots you don't take."

-Wayne Gretzky

"If you aren't going all the way, why go at all?"

-Joe Namath

SECTION #3
THE GOOGLE
BLUEPRINT

CAPTURE MORE OPPORTUNITIES BY CONSISTENTLY TESTING YOUR ADS & UTILIZING THE RIGHT AD FORMATS.

You'll Discover How To Increase Your Conversions By Testing Ad Copy, Increase Your Response Rates, Show Off The Best Parts Of Your Business With New Ad Formats, And Watch Your Competition Through The Ad Preview Tool.

PLAY #27 | Improve Response Rates By Creating Ads that Satisfy the Buyers Search Intent

Play Action:

Develop and Implement Ads That Satisfy The Search Intentions of The Buyer.

If a buyer types "tankless water heater installation" into Google there's a good chance they're looking to purchase and have installed a tankless water heater. Most advertisers make the mistake of either trying to do too much or not putting in the required amount of effort to build out an ad that speaks directly to the intention of their buyer.

fig. 27-1

In the example to the left *(fig 27-1)*, I typed, "tankless water heater" into Google. You can see the 4th ad down doesn't even mention tankless water heating. It's a generic ad from my local utility company in the Boston area, National Grid, offering a gas heating rebate.

If I click on the ad it takes me to *(fig 27-2)* a no-cost home energy assessment. Nowhere on the page does it even have the slightest mention of a tankless water heater. In this case, the utility company is going to have a very low click-through rate and extremely low conversion and return on their ad spend because the sales funnel they built does not align to the search intent.

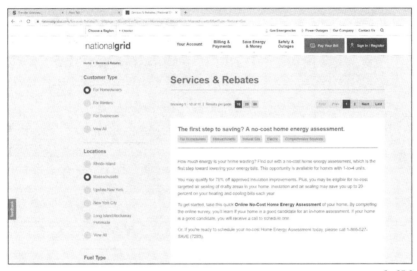

fig. 27-2

There is an intention the buyer comes to the table with when they search on Google. Look closely at your keywords and make sure you have ads and landing pages that satisfy what a searcher is looking for when they type that term in. When you create an offer, a call to action, and implement your targeted ad copy you'll satisfy the buyer intent and increase your chances of a relevant click.

To Summarize:

○ Give the buyer exactly what they are looking for.

○ Make it simple and don't over complicate it. Focus on the service the customer is looking for.

Play #27 / Improve Response Rates By Creating Ads that Satisfy Intent

✗   Make your message clear.

◯   Give them a direct path to reach you.

✗   Provide a specific offer that is relevant to that search term.

Google gives you the ability to break down campaigns and create custom ads specific to a keyword. Invest the time, effort, and energy and you'll increase click-through and conversion rates giving the buyer exactly what they came to search for.

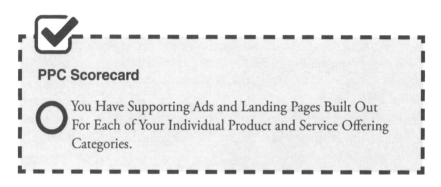

PPC Scorecard

◯ You Have Supporting Ads and Landing Pages Built Out For Each of Your Individual Product and Service Offering Categories.

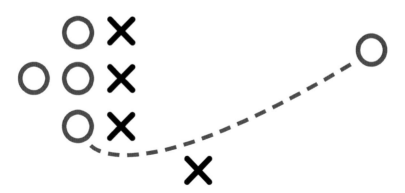

Play #27 / Improve Response Rates By Creating Ads that Satisfy Intent

PLAY #28 | How Increasing Your Click-Through Rates Will Help You Drive Down Costs

Play Action:

Work on Improving Your Click-Through Rate to Increase Response Rates and Drive Down Costs.

Your click-through rate (CTR) is the percentage of people who take action and click on your ads divided by the total number of impressions (or views) your ads received. So if your ad received 100 impressions and 25 clicks you would have a 25% click-through rate.

Click-through rate is a measurement of how well your campaigns are optimized. This includes your keyword portfolio, your campaign settings, along with the quality and engagement of your ad copy. It's a health score really. If you suffer from low click-through rate you usually have a lot of broad keywords driving in irrelevant traffic. Your ads might also not be appealing enough or not speaking directly to the buyer's intent. You may also have an issue with your campaign settings. Or perhaps it's a combination of all of these issues.

The higher your click-through rate the higher your quality score will be. For that reason, you'll start enjoying the benefit of a lower cost per click and better ad position. Since you'll have higher click efficiency you'll enjoy the added benefit of a higher impression share, too. Below is a summary of how to improve your CTR and enjoy the benefits of this increased metric.

The best ways to improve your CTR:

- O   Split test your ad copy to see if one version performs better.
- O   Follow the Ad Copy Formula.
- ✗   Eliminate non-performing keywords.
- O   Put keywords into S.K.A.G.S (single keyword ad groups).

 Steve's PPC Breakdown:

Where Do You Begin to Improve CTR?

In a larger account where you may have hundreds or thousands of keywords the best place to begin making click-through rate improvements are with the keywords that receive the most impressions. Go to the keywords section and extend the date range of your view to "all time". Here you are going to get a bird's eye view into your market over a period of time. Sort your keywords by impression counts, starting with the keywords that get the most traffic. If you have many impressions but no clicks, your keywords are most likely not supported with enough negative keywords or your ads might not be descriptive enough. Look at both of these angles as you go down the list and make the necessary improvements. Work only the keywords that have received more than 100 search impressions.

You'll find that all of your actions and positive consequences are connected. As you start to increase your click-through rate, your conversion rate will rise as well, helping you generate more leads without spending more.

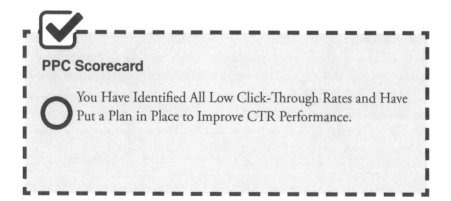

PPC Scorecard

O   You Have Identified All Low Click-Through Rates and Have Put a Plan in Place to Improve CTR Performance.

PLAY #29

Increase Conversion Rates with Consistent Ad Copy Split Testing By Using Google Ad Variations

Play Action:

Work on Improving Your Ad Copy Response Rates By Continuously Testing Slight Variations of Your Messaging.

Does the ad headline "Same Day Service" or "60-Minute Service" drive in more leads? With Google Ad Variations you'll be able to find out.

You can easily test your messaging by using Google Ad Variations. Ad Variations is a tool within your Google account that allows you to easily create and test different versions of your ads across your campaigns and entire account. Essentially, you're running an experiment to see how people react to the words you use, the call to actions, and offers you have been running in your ads.

You'll see which version of an ad delivers a better result when you compare click-through rate performance. From there you can pick the winning version and implement it across a campaign. It's this process of testing and refinement that will help you get more for less.

Consistently testing and fine tuning the language you use in your ads will help you increase your click-through rate (or CTR.) This will increase and improve your quality scores which reduces your overall cost per click and as a result will deliver more ads. All this is to say, you'll yield higher conversions and more leads when you run the best version of your ad copy.

If you want to ensure that the best, most enticing messaging is in front of your customers, you should be using the Ad Variations tool regularly.

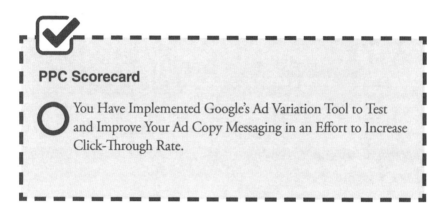

PPC Scorecard

You Have Implemented Google's Ad Variation Tool to Test and Improve Your Ad Copy Messaging in an Effort to Increase Click-Through Rate.

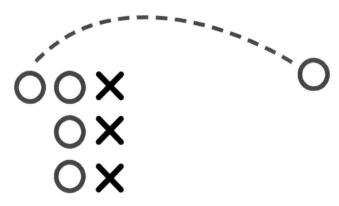

Play #29 / Increase Conversion Rates with Consistent Ad Copy

PLAY #30 | Build a Bigger and Better Ad Using Google's Expanded Text Ads

Play Action:

Attract Your Best Customers By Implementing Google's Expanded Text Ads. Use All Available Real Estate to Build a Compelling Message That Stands Out From The Crowd.

If you advertised more than 10 years ago, you may remember the flashy, attention-getting style of Google ads alerting anyone who saw them of what they were. Just a few years ago, you may recall seeing ads on the right hand side of a Google search page. Once again, Google has changed how the search results page appears.

Today, ads now blend seamlessly into the page (much like an organic listing) making viewers want to click on them. The designation of ads are mentioned with just a small bubble next to the link. If it wasn't for that bubble, it wouldn't appear to be an ad at all. Just like that, smarter consumers who may not have clicked on your ad before are now interested in your business because Google has done a good job of making ads look similar to the organic listings.

At the same time, Google is giving you, the advertiser, more real estate to use with new and improved **Expanded Text Ads:**

O   You now have three headlines you can work with instead of two. The first two headlines are required, while the third is optional-however, I highly recommend you use all three. Each headline includes a 30-character limit. The headlines are separated by a vertical pipe ("I"). The headlines are flexible in that they wrap to a second line based on the size of the prospects screen.

O   Below the headline you have two 90-character description fields. This gives you a lot more height and room to work with in expanding your message.

X   Your display URL can include two optional "path" fields. The text you place in the path fields do not have to be the exact URL, rather you can work in descriptive text that may play a part in your core offer messaging.

O   You no longer have to create ads just for mobile devices. Expanded text ads work on both desktop and mobile.

LASIK As Low As $220/eye | Affordable LASIK
Near You | LASIKVisionInstitute.com

Over 1.3 Million Surgeries Performed. Largest U.S. LASIK
Provider. Free Consultation. Over 15 Years Of LASIK
Experience. Great Financing Available. The Latest LASIK
Technology. Affordable Pricing. Latest LASIK Technology.
Convenient Locations.

fig. 27-1: Expanded text ad

With Google's expanded text ads you'll have more freedom with your text to create unique ads that attract fresh high quality leads. Here's a great example of a laser eye surgery center taking advantage of Google's Expanded Text Ads.

At the core of what Expanded Text Ads has to offer is control and the opportunity to build out and communicate a better message leading to more qualified leads.

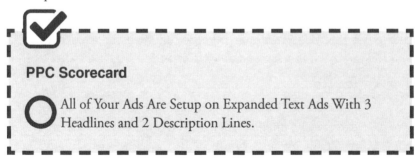

PPC Scorecard

O   All of Your Ads Are Setup on Expanded Text Ads With 3 Headlines and 2 Description Lines.

PLAY **#31** | ## How Google is Helping Advertisers Improve Advertising Performance With NEW Responsive Search Ads

Play Action:

Implement Google's New Responsive Search Ads to Achieve a Higher Click-Through Rate and Reduced Cost Per Click.

Responsive Search Ads, one of Google's newest innovations, are designed to help you improve ad performance. With Responsive Ads Google is able to automatically learn which components of your ads work and get the best performance. They are designed to help you build more successful, better performing ads.

With responsive ads you can write up to 15 different headlines and 4 descriptions that Google will pull from. These headlines and descriptions can then be arranged into over 43,000 unique combinations! With Google at the wheel automatically assessing how your ads are doing, your content will be adapted to fit your customers' search terms automatically with each new search. Google will learn what combinations perform best and serve those ads to customers more frequently. Responsive Search Ads are a phenomenal tool for presenting your best ads without having to test thousands of combinations yourself. It puts powerful machine learning technology into the hands of even the smallest advertiser.

Part of what the machine does with responsive ads is to automatically deliver an ad based on the combinations you already setup. If you're concerned that an important part of your ad will disappear while changing combinations, keep in mind you can always pin what you want to keep. In fact, a great way to switch over to responsive ads is by taking what works from your current ads and bringing it over as the starting point. Be wary of pinning too often though, as it severely limits Google's ability to test what's working with ad combinations.

Steve's PPC Breakdown:

At the time of writing this book, Responsive Search Ads were being offered to advertisers in BETA, which means you may not have access to this feature until it is released to all advertisers. As a Google Premier Partner one of the benefits my clients receive is the ability to enroll in these new features.

From the testing I've done on responsive ads, I've seen an impressive increase in overall click-through rates. 66% of the tests I am currently conducting are generating a lower cost per click as well with no change in cost per lead performance. This basically means Responsive Search Ads are helping to capture more relevant traffic at a reduced rate without an increase to lead costs.

Remember that your Responsive Search Ad may not show all 3 headlines and 2 descriptions if it's being viewed on a smaller screen. However, it will always show 2 headlines.

Don't forget to add some creativity to your headlines. Not only should you avoid boring headlines if you're hoping to catch the eye of your audience, but Google actually won't show your responsive search ad if your headlines are too similar. Create a variety of options that have the message you want to deliver without repeating the same phrasing.

Through the help of machine learning, Google can continually test your ads for what works, scrap what doesn't work, and move you towards creating ads that attract higher quality leads.

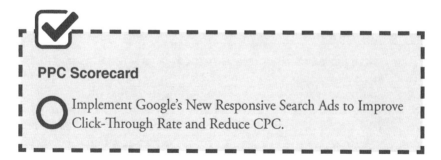

PPC Scorecard

Implement Google's New Responsive Search Ads to Improve Click-Through Rate and Reduce CPC.

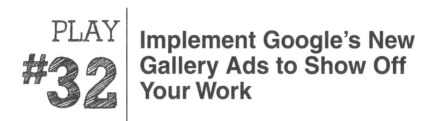

PLAY #32 | **Implement Google's New Gallery Ads to Show Off Your Work**

Play Action:

If You Sell a Service or Product with a Pleasing Visual Outcome You Can Implement Google's New Gallery Ads to Show Off Your Pictures and Appeal to the Visual Buyer.

Looking to attract your "visual thinker" audience? Until now, there's been a gap in this type of marketing in Google's search platform. Luckily, this is where gallery ads excel.

With the rise in popularity of visual media like Snapchat, Instagram, and Facebook it's important to meet your audience where they are. Currently, gallery ads are only available for mobile devices which makes sense for the visual customer that is using these other apps. The rise of mobile use has been swift and seemingly nonstop.

Gallery ads are a visually enticing, swipe-able ad format that allows you to use a minimum of 4 images and a maximum of 8 images, along with a 70 character description, and 3 headlines (just like expanded text ads) to engage your audience. Each individual image also comes with a tagline.

The human brain processes imagery 60,000x faster than text. The potential with gallery ads is obvious. Yet, it doesn't seem that all businesses lend themselves to visual ads. How can you use this new type of ad to your advantage no matter what services you offer, even if they're not the most glamorous?

Let's look at an example. If you're a dentist looking to try gallery ads but don't think pictures of someone getting a root canal are going to reel in clients… you'd be right.

Instead, try picturing the benefits of using your service:

- O   A person with white, clean teeth.
- O   A team of trusted professionals combined with stats about your years of service.
- O   A side by side comparison before and after of some of the work you've done.
- X   An image representing the link between a healthy heart and dental health.

By providing pictures of the benefits rather than the features you'll be able to help your prospects imagine the positive results of using your services. Gallery ads are a powerful advertising weapon to yield and you don't want to miss out.

What are you waiting for? Choose your most exciting photos, set up your gallery ads before your competitors, and reap the benefits of creative advertising.

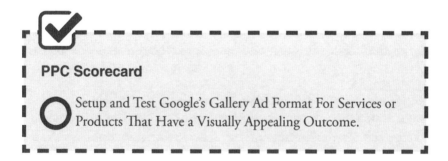

PPC Scorecard

O   Setup and Test Google's Gallery Ad Format For Services or Products That Have a Visually Appealing Outcome.

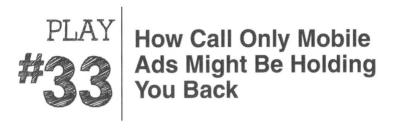

PLAY #33 | **How Call Only Mobile Ads Might Be Holding You Back**

Play Action:

Evaluate Your Mobile Advertising Strategy. If You Are Currently Using Call Only Ads, Test Them Against Expanded Text Ads to See Which Ad Format Delivers a Better Result.

Call only ads are designed to encourage people to call your business right from their phone. They appear only on devices that make phone calls such as smartphones and tablets with phone call features. When a potential customer clicks on your ad, the ad places a call to you directly from their device.

You won't find this ad format available on desktop. These ads are designed specifically for mobile display which is a smaller piece of ad real estate. Because of this, it's possible that in certain cases some of the information you were trying to convey may not show depending on the size of the screen. This means you need to be strategic about what information you place in your ad copy.

Steve's PPC Breakdown

By the nature of call only ads, a prospect is forced to call you directly which bypasses the landing page experience. I'm not a fan of this ad format for that exact reason. Bypassing the landing page eliminates the buyers ability to get more details, establish trust, and gain confidence in your company

Steve's PPC Breakdown *(continued)*

or brand. Lead conversion happens on the landing page. I have personally seen decreased conversion rates with this type of ad format with my own testing. I do see what Google is trying to accomplish- skipping a step to streamline the buyers experience- however I think this ad format is a little ahead of its time and **can hurt your performance**.

Every interaction a prospect has with your brand is a step towards building trust in your company. In turn, a lack of interactions can greatly reduce your conversion rate. The absence of details given to your prospect with call only ads leaves them missing key information about your offer, too. By limiting the buyer's interactions you're limiting the buyer's experience with your brand and lowering their likelihood to interact with you.

If you insist upon implementing call only ads or if you're running them today, I'd highly recommend testing them against expanded text ads with call extensions. This setup gives the buyer an option to click on your ad to learn more about your company by going to a landing page along with giving them an option to call right from the ad. It's the best of both worlds.

Even though they are call only ads, you'll still be paying for clicks, not just for successful calls. This type of ad format will help your competitors get your clicks and take business away from you.

Make sure you test this campaign type prior to committing to it.

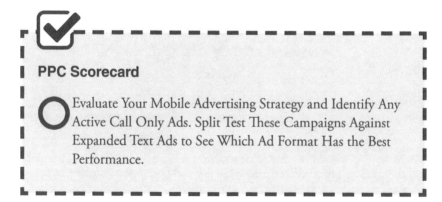

PPC Scorecard

Evaluate Your Mobile Advertising Strategy and Identify Any Active Call Only Ads. Split Test These Campaigns Against Expanded Text Ads to See Which Ad Format Has the Best Performance.

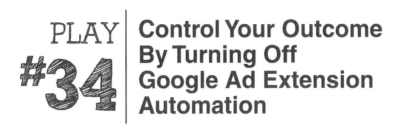

PLAY #34 | **Control Your Outcome By Turning Off Google Ad Extension Automation**

Play Action:

Shut Off Google Ad Extension Automation That Will Hurt Your Advertising Performance.

Google's search campaign setup now includes automated extensions. It's Google's automatic way of beefing up your ads based on your goals, your website information, and other factors. The challenge here is that it's 100% automated and done by a machine, with no human input as to what extensions get chosen.

Most extensions show on all ad types with the exception of a few that will only show on desktop. When an automated extension is predicted to improve your ad's performance, Google Ads automatically creates it and shows it below the current ad.

The trouble with this happening by itself is that Google may pull in messaging that doesn't make sense with your ads. It could pull old information from your site or an expired offer.

To turn off automated extensions:

1. Go to Search Campaigns
2. Ads and extensions
3. Click "Automated Extensions"
4. Click "More"
5. Then click "Advanced Options"
6. Turn off the specific automated extensions

How would you like automated extensions to work in your account?

○ Use all automated extensions that typically boost ads' performance ⊙
   Best option for most advertisers

◉ Turn off specific automated extensions
   Not recommended because it could negatively affect your ads' performance

Currently off for this account:

(Automated location extensions ⊗) (Dynamic structured snippets ⊗) (Dynamic callouts ⊗) (Dynamic sitelinks ⊗)

(Automated app extensions ⊗)

Turn off automated extension

Select which extension to turn off

Seller ratings
Longer ad headlines
Automated call extensions

fig. 34-1: Turn off Google Ad extension automation

I recommend shutting off all automated extensions and setting up extensions manually with the exception of the following:

- ○ Seller Ratings.
- ○ Call Extensions.
- ✗ Longer Headlines.

These extensions will always work with your messaging, regardless of ad copy or offer. They will not hurt your performance the way other automated ad extensions do.

Take control of your ads again by turning off automated extensions. This allows you to fully customize your message and ensure the right information is being presented to your customers.

PPC Scorecard

○ You Have Shut Off Google Ad Extension Automation to Prevent Poor Ad Quality.

PLAY

#35

Discover A Simple Fix To Stop Losing Business Over Phone Numbers

Play Action:

Shut Off Google Call Automation to Control The Phone Lines Your Potential Customers See and Interact With.

People hang onto phone numbers, especially if they are considering doing business with you. Make sure you own your call tracking lines and don't rely on Google to populate them for you.

As mentioned previously in this book, using local phone lines when targeting a local audience is best practice. Turn off Google call reporting when setting up your call extensions to ensure a customer is being served a phone line with the area code you want.

Google call reporting will serve up a Google phone number that they own- it doesn't belong to you and there's a good chance it will be an 800 number. 800 numbers are off-putting to customers and distance you as a local service provider. The last time I checked, ads were being associated with toll-free 833 numbers. If you're like me, 833 doesn't feel like a toll free number.

You can find this setting in your account settings under "Call Reporting".

fig. 35-1: Call reporting

You want to track your calls using a call tracking solution where **you own your local lines and have control over them.** You'll be able to record calls to improve call performance, track the quality of your leads, and track which marketing campaigns are providing you with quality leads all while appearing local to all your prospects.

PPC Scorecard

○   You Have Shut Off Automated Google Call Reporting to Prevent Loss of Future Call Opportunities and to Provide Buyers With a Local Line They Trust.

Play #35 / Discover A Simple Fix To Stop Losing Business Over Phone Numbers

PLAY #36 | Using the Google Ad Preview Tool to Spy on Competitors

Play Action:

Evaluate Competitor Movement in Your Market on a Monthly Cycle By Taking a Snapshot of Your Market Everyday.

Have you ever wanted to see what type of offers your competitors are running? Want to know the time of day when they start and stop showing ads, leaving you an opportunity to score big?

See which position your ads are in compared to your competitor's using Google's Ad Preview tool. Evaluate the competitions ad copy to see what they're offering in their ads so you can remain competitive and in the game.

When do your competitors drop off and run out of budget? See if there's a certain time of day when your competitor falls off and strategize to capture those opportunities. This could be a sign of poor budget management on their part, which you can use to your advantage. Pay close attention not only to certain times of day but to certain days throughout the month.

Knowing when your competitors come in and out can help you take advantage of the "off times" to generate leads at a discount. All of this can be accomplished through the Ad Preview Tool in Google.

I like to capture a screenshot of the market and put them into a PowerPoint document. At the end of the month I can evaluate who is in the game and who is out. At the same time, I can evaluate who is actively making changes to bidding and ad copy.

Note: Searching for your own ads on a live Google search will not give you the true representation of what is happening in the market. The Google Ads Preview Tool will give you the <u>most accurate read on your market</u> because the live Google search takes into consideration your search history, device history, IP address, cookies in your browser and other factors that will skew your personalized search results.

 Steve's PPC Breakdown

Does your ad positioning fluctuate throughout the day? You can identify a competitor who is stuck in a "set and forget" Google setup and has automated bidding in place. Here's how…

Take a high volume keyword and increase it to, let's say $100. If the competitor automatically outranks you within a few minutes of making the adjustment than you know they are in an automated bidding position. There is no one looking out for them.

Use With Caution- If you have a large enough budget you can inflate your competitors costs considerably ultimately knocking them out of the game by increasing your bid rate to an obscenely large number. You'll see how fast your competitor falls off the page as their budget is exhausted.

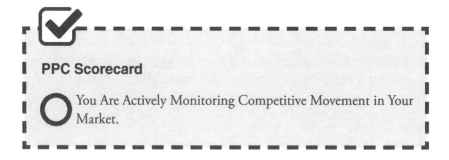

PPC Scorecard

You Are Actively Monitoring Competitive Movement in Your Market.

"When you've got something to prove, there's nothing greater than a challenge."

-Terry Bradshaw

"I've failed over and over and over again in my life. And that is why I succeed."

-Michael Jordan

SECTION #4 GOOGLE AD EXTENSIONS

GIVE YOUR ADS A BOOST BY IMPLEMENTING THE BEST AD EXTENSIONS FOR YOUR BUSINESS.

You'll Learn How To Increase Your Ad Real Estate, Attract The Right Customers, Drive In More Relevant Traffic, Show Off Your Business, And Increase Your Click-Through Rate With Google's Wide Variety Of Ad Extensions.

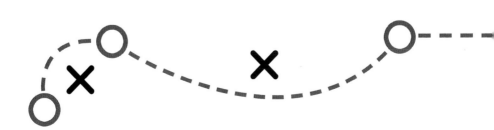

PLAY #37

Stand Out From The Crowd with Google's Callout Extensions

Play Action:

Implement Callout Extensions to Support Your Primary Google Ad and Boost Your Response Rates with This Additional Advertising Real Estate.

Chances are you are not the only business in your area that specializes in a particular service. You know what makes your company better than your competitors- but is that clear to potential customers? Don't become just another dime a dozen. Make sure you use callout extensions to stand out.

Callout extensions are an optional line of text you can add to your Google ad. They give you the ability to communicate supporting messages that did not make it into your primary ad copy.

I like to work in differentiating statements about my clients in my callout extensions.

Implementing this feature doesn't cost you anything extra but the benefit is an improved CTR. With callouts you are increasing the height of your ads. I've seen ads get an immediate 10% bump in response rates when using these ad extensions. Callout extensions are extremely flexible, too. You can schedule them to run at specific times with custom scheduling which gives you the ability to put out the right message, at the right time, in front of the right audience. You can also restrict them to run on mobile devices only.

Here are a few different example callout applications so you can get an idea on how you would use them for your business:

Highlight Sales and Deals

> *Ex.* 20% Off Bathtub Installation This Month, Free Extended Warranty

Build Trust

> *Ex.* Local Since 1978, Family Owned, 24-Hr Live Answer, Immediate Service, 5-Star Reviews

Showcase Inventory, Expertise

> *Ex.* All Sizes In Stock, Bathtub Remodeling Specialist

You can add as many callout extensions to your campaign as you would like. Between 2-6 callout extensions can appear on your ad when it appears on desktop or mobile. Each callout has a 25-character limit, but I recommend that you keep them short. Use no more than 15 characters so they are succinct and clear. You want them to help your primary offer, not distract buyers away from the ad so create them at the adgroup level. This gives you the ability to customize callouts for each unique ad set.

Here are a few other tips and tricks for making the most out of your callout extensions:

Follow Google Ads Callout Requirements

Make sure you are following Google's guidelines or else your callout will be disapproved:

- O   No punctuation or symbols
- O   No repetition in your ad copy
- ✗   No trademarks

Capitalize First Letter Of Every Word

Get people to look at your callouts and make them look professional by capitalizing the first letter of every word.

Create At Least Four

You should have no less than four callout extensions for each of your ads. Make the most out of that valuable free real estate you're getting from Google.

Callout extensions are a great way to highlight everything that makes your ad special. If you want to make the most of your ads, this should be one of the first extensions you use.

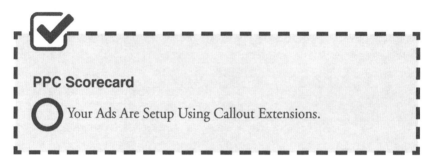

PPC Scorecard

Your Ads Are Setup Using Callout Extensions.

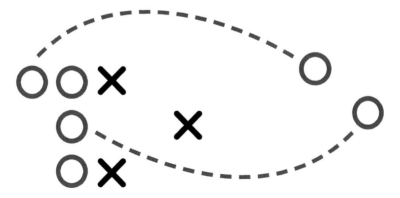

Play #37 / Stand Out From The Crowd with Google's Callout Extensions

PLAY
#38

How To Generate More Phone Leads with Google Call Extensions

Play Action:

Implement Call Extensions in Your Campaigns Using Your Local Call Tracking Lines to Generate More Local Phone Call Leads.

In my opinion, a lead that comes to you by way of a phone call from a prospect is the strongest type of lead. In fact, 90% of the leads I generate for my clients are phone leads. If you want to turn clicks into phone calls then you should make sure you are using call extensions within the Google Ads account for your business.

Call extensions are a type of ad extension that allows you to put your phone numbers in your ad for a prospect to call you directly.

fig. 38-1: Example of call extension

Call extensions are great for improving response rates and are very easy to implement into your campaigns and ads. Call extensions add another component to your ad to help it stand out in a crowded market.

You can run call extensions using Google provided phone lines or by adding your own lines. I recommend you use your own lines because the phone numbers that use local area codes for each area you serve will get better response rates. When you use trusted call tracking systems you can often get detailed analytics about each call you get as well. The upside is you actually own your call tracking lines.

When you use Google's call tracking lines, you're not always guaranteed to serve a local line and you don't own the numbers. Sometimes you will see 800 numbers pop up. Sometimes those numbers will change, so if a customer writes a number down to call later you might lose that client.

Since these can be added at the campaign or ad group level, you can set call extensions to run only during your hours of operation and you can assign different numbers to different campaigns. This comes in handy when you service a large market with different local lines.

The cost model to use call extensions is the same as a click. If someone clicks on your phone line in an ad you will be charged as if they clicked on the ad itself. Using the call extension feature does not inflate your price.

Like other ad extensions there is no guarantee that your call extensions will show. Those are usually reserved for the top-ranked ads. To give yourself the best chance of having your call extension appear make sure you are bidding competitively and using well written ad copy to fight for top ad rank. The more you are willing to spend on a click, the more ad extension features will appear.

Call extensions are a great way to get to the heart of your main objective for using Google Ads– to get the phone ringing.

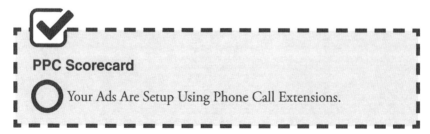

PPC Scorecard

Your Ads Are Setup Using Phone Call Extensions.

PLAY #39 | # How To Enhance Your Ads & Own More Google Advertising Real Estate

Play Action:

Implement Sitelinks on Your Google Ads to Enhance Your Message and Increase Response Rates.

Putting together an ad is kind of like putting together an outfit. Your headline is your shirt. Your description is your pants. Your URL is your pair of shoes. But now you want to dress it up with a nice jacket, or some flashy cufflinks. That is where ad extensions come in. In this section, I'm going to be discussing sitelinks.

Sitelinks make it easy for people to navigate to your website by providing links to specific pages. They are the blue links you see below an ad. These can be links to services you want to highlight, or a page highlighting why a customer should choose your business, or your company's blog. It's completely up to you.

I recommend you use sitelinks to strengthen your offer by positioning your added value and guarantee. It's also a great spot to sprinkle in financing offers, offers during holidays and offers for weather-driven events.

Here are a few reasons why you should be taking advantage of sitelink extensions.

O   They don't cost anything extra. You are only charged per click like you would be with any other ad.

○ They are flexible. You can time sitelinks to run on a certain day, during specific times and can end them at anytime. You can build different sitelinks for each of your campaigns or ad groups.

✗ More ad space real estate for you. They add another level of height to your ad. As a result you'll take up more space in a competitive situation, making them more enticing to potential customers. Increasing the height of your ads will ultimately boost your click-through rates.

Here is an example of a business using sitelink extensions:

Cleaning Service From $23/Hr - First 3-Hour Cleaning For $35
[Ad] www.handy.com/Cleaning ▾
4.2 ★★★★☆ rating for handy.com
Book Local, Trusted **Cleaners** Instantly on Your Phone. Multiple Plans Available.
Trusted Professionals · 300k 5-Star Ratings · Next-Day Availability · 3.5M+ Cleanings Completed
Services: Home Cleaning, Furniture Assembly, TV Mounting

    15% Off Handyman Services   TV Mounting
    Professional Moving Help

fig. 39-1: Ad with sitelink extension

They are on the same search page above this ad for a business providing the same service:

The Maids Cleaning Service - Nobody Cleans Like The Maids
[Ad] www.themaidsma.com/CleaningService/$25Voucher ▾
Call Now For A Free Estimate & Save $25 Off Your **Cleaning Service** From The Maids

fig. 39-2: Ad without sitelink extension

You can see the difference in how much space the top ad gets compared to the competitor below.

Sitelinks are proven to increase CTR by 10-20%.

Sitelink extensions are a great way to make your ad experience better for potential customers by directing them to exactly where they want to go. The best way to optimize them is by keeping them specific to your core offer and in alignment with the buyer's search intent.

Your ad can show up to 8 sitelinks on a mobile or tablet device and up to 6 on desktop search. The sitelink headline can be no more than 25 characters and you get two description lines both 35 characters in length. Here's what the sitelink interface looks like.

fig. 39-3: Sitelink interface

Here are some tips and tricks for using sitelink extensions:

Up Your Ad Rank

There is no guarantee that sitelink extensions will appear since Google chooses when they will show. However, ads that are ranked higher are proven to show more sitelink extensions. Improving your ad rank and increasing your bids will give you the best chance that your extensions will appear in a search.

Keep it Succinct

Even though you have a 25-character limit, Google recommends you only use 18-20 characters for desktop sitelink extensions and 12-15 for mobile sitelink extensions. That way you can make sure that the entire sitelink will show instead of seeing a dreaded "…" showing up in the middle of your ad.

Keep Tabs on Extensions

Periodically check on your extensions to make sure they are not linking potential customers to broken pages.

Don't Repeat Yourself

Make sure you don't repeat the same terms in your sitelink extensions that you do in your description lines. Take advantage of your extra space by using unique phrases throughout your ad.

Pay Close Attention To Google's Policy

It is important to not just glance over Google's policy on sitelink extensions. If they do not meet requirements, they will never show up. Stick to the rules and make sure your sitelink extensions adhere to the following:

- ○ No duplicate URL's.
- ○ No third-party URL's.
- ✗ No punctuations and symbols (keep your exclamation points away!)
- ○ No link text repetition.

Sitelink extensions can be a great way to boost your ad once you know how to make them work for your business.

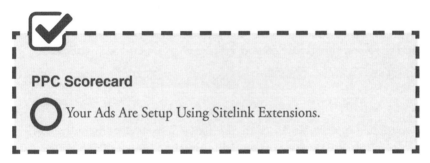

PPC Scorecard

○ Your Ads Are Setup Using Sitelink Extensions.

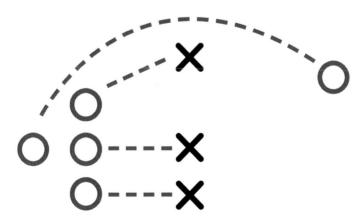

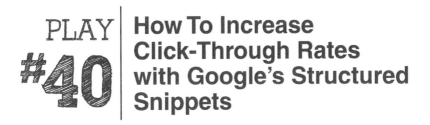

PLAY #40 | **How To Increase Click-Through Rates with Google's Structured Snippets**

Play Action:

Implement Structured Snippets on Your Google Ads to Provide Details About Your Specific Products and Services.

You can think of structured snippets as the hot fudge on top of your ad sundae. They don't change what's going on with the ad, they just provide some much needed emphasis to make it even better.

Structured snippets are ad extensions that work to highlight specific things about your product or service in a way that's quick to read, customizable, and provides additional detail to your viewers.

They are designed to help people find out more about your products and services as a whole. As an advertiser, Google gives you the ability to give potential customers a supporting list or details that bolster your core offering.

For example:

If you are in the market to further your education, a college may use the "Degree programs" structured snippets to outline the types of degrees they offer ie. Bachelors, Masters, PhD. The goal when using them is to provide a deeper level of context to your ad viewers. Best of all, they're simple to use.

Google provides you the following categories where you can setup the structured snippet ad extension feature:

- O Amenities
- O Brands
- ✕ Courses
- O Degree Programs
- O Destinations
- ✕ Featured Hotels
- ✕ Insurance Coverage

- O Models
- O Neighborhoods
- ✕ Service Catalog
- O Shows
- O Styles
- O Types

Start by choosing the header that corresponds with the values you plan on choosing.

For example, if you're a travel company talking about all the places your clients can fly to you'd select the header "Destinations" so you could input locations as your values. If you're a cosmetic surgeon your header might be "Services" so you can input values that reflect your specific services like "Facelifts," "Tummy Tucks," etc. Here's an example of what a structured snippet looks like:

fig. 40-1: Structured snippet example

You can add structured snippets at the account, campaign, or adgroup level and even schedule when you'd like them to show. Be sure to add your snippets wisely by following a few rules of thumb:

Know Your Audience- Most users will be viewing your ads through mobile devices so keep your snippets shorter rather than longer and plan for how they'll look on mobile.

Decide on How Many- Plan to have at least 4 snippets per header to give your viewer enough info about your company.

Be Precise- Unlike callout extensions which highlight a single part of your business, snippets are meant to describe the totality of a group of products or services you provide.

With a structured snippet your prospect will immediately learn more about what you're offering in a way that's easily digestible. Having this information will take your ad to the next level and increase your click through rate.

The more your viewers know about your service the greater chance your company is going to stand out. Using this tool will help you with increasing your click-through rates.

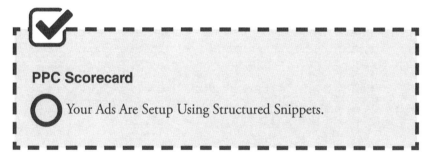

PPC Scorecard

◯ Your Ads Are Setup Using Structured Snippets.

Play Action:

Implement Message Extensions on Mobile Ads to Connect With Prospects Faster.

The future is mobile. The average person currently spends over 3 hours on their phone a day. This amount of time is expected to increase in the years to come and Google has designed a number of mobile features that they've made available in Google Ads. The feature we are talking about in this chapter is Message Extensions.

Message Extensions are another way to communicate with your future customers faster than ever before right in the palm of their hand. With a message extension your mobile prospects can click on your extension right in the ad and be led to a pre-populated message in their texting app.

Instead of driving a phone call it drives a **text conversation**.

With younger generations trending away from making phone calls, this extension can be especially useful to reach generations that might not respond to other attempts at a call to action. Don't worry if you're not a big texter yourself- this extension has you covered, too.

You can choose how you wish to receive your messages and the responses will still be received in the form of a text by your prospects. Choose a phone number to receive your messages on your mobile phone or choose email forwarding to receive them in the form of an email.

Say you're running a special for new customers but you want them to be able to ask any questions they have. At the end of your ad you may include a "Text" button they can click on to reach out to your company quickly. You'll be charged for this click the same way as if a prospect had clicked on an ad that led them to your website. Message extensions are an easy way for both parties to communicate effectively.

If you're worried about being too busy to receive the volume of message responses you're anticipating, creating an email alias will forward the messages to a group of people of your choosing. You can get your whole team in on the process if necessary.

Here's an example of my company AdMachines using message extensions to answer questions from potential customers:

fig. 41-1: Message extension - desktop

Let your potential customers communicate with your business directly through your ads for a faster, more efficient path to your sale.

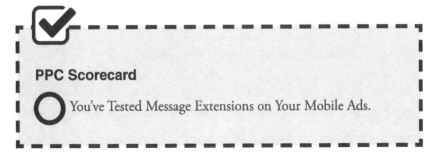

PPC Scorecard

You've Tested Message Extensions on Your Mobile Ads.

PLAY
#42

How To Drive More Traffic to Your Business Using Location Extensions

Play Action:

Implement Location Extensions to Make it Easier for Shoppers to Find Your Location.

One of the most important aspects of potential customers using your services and buying your products is also the simplest; they have to be able to find you.

Over 20% of Google searches are for local products, services, or places. With a location extension your business information including your address, phone number, and a map marker will show up with your ad. The easier it is to locate your services, the more people will contact you. See the example below of what a location extension looks like.

fig. 42-1: Location extensions

There are two types of location extensions:

1. **Google Ad Location Extensions** - These help people find your business using your address, a map, and their distance from your business. It's useful to draw customers right to your home base if you have a retail business location.

2. **Affiliate Location Extensions** - Helps prospects find local stores that sell your products. This is really helpful if you're trying to build your business through partnerships with retail chains.

In addition location extensions have several different features on desktop and mobile including:

○ Showing the distance to your location and its city (mobile).

○ Displaying your location's street address (computer).

○ An easy way for potential customers to call you with a clickable "Call" button (mobile).

○ A tappable or clickable access to a details page for your location with information such as hours, phone number, photos, and driving directions.

If you have multiple locations, all of your locations will show up along with the distance it would take the viewer to get to each one. Location extensions make it as simple as possible for people to buy your products and use your services.

It's even possible to record your success rate at the location extension level through location reporting. You'll be able to measure the online conversions per location if you have more than one.

Steve's PPC Breakdown

Now location extensions are really useful for retailers and those businesses that drive traffic to their brick and mortar location. If you own a service-based business and travel to the locations of your customers, then you want to carefully consider how you would use this ad extension. It can definitely act as a trust builder in your local city, however if you travel long distances from your location to service customers then you would basically be advertising the fact that you are not a local provider. It displays your business address information right in the ad, so in this scenario location extensions can hurt your response rates.

Keep in mind you can assign location extensions at the campaign level giving you the ultimate flexibility in controlling how they appear on specific campaigns.

NOTE: In order to implement Google location settings you need a Google My Business account and active profile. This account will link with your Google Ads account. This is where your location details feed from so make sure they are up to date.

If you're looking to grow your business by driving foot traffic to your location and you want to help customers use your service with ease, make sure you're utilizing the location extension tool in your ads.

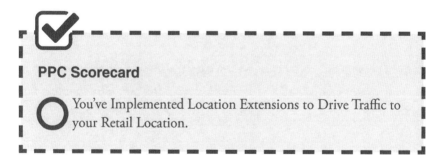

PPC Scorecard

O You've Implemented Location Extensions to Drive Traffic to your Retail Location.

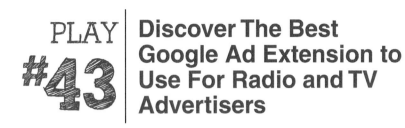

PLAY #43 | Discover The Best Google Ad Extension to Use For Radio and TV Advertisers

Play Action:

Implement Price Extensions to Protect Your Branded Traffic.

As I'm writing this chapter, I am actually implementing price extensions for one of my long time home services clients who repairs and installs heating and cooling equipment. This particular company runs a lot of TV and radio ads in addition to advertising on Google. In their TV commercials they are positioning direct offers and pricing for air conditioner repairs, replacement and maintenance.

Over the years I have worked with many companies that launch multi-media campaigns and when they do there is always a significant increase in their branded search on Google. A percentage of interested prospects who see the TV commercial or hear the radio spot naturally go right to Google and search the company information. Launching a branded campaign using price extensions is a great way to capture this traffic and protect it so it doesn't go to your competitors.

Price extensions are a type of ad extension that lets you add a set of rows to the bottom of your ad that highlights the prices or deals for different services you provide.

Here I am showing you the offers my client is running on same day AC repairs, the price for a new central air system, and the price for an AC tune-up:

Same Day Repairs	New Central Air	21-Point AC Tune-Up
$59	$5,995	$97
Off any A/C repair	14 Ton, 3 Seer System	Cleaning & Check-up

fig. 43-1: Price extensions

Steve's PPC Breakdown

Now, in order to use price extensions you are required to add a minimum of at least three offers with a maximum of eight. As many as five can be displayed in the search results at any given time. However, you can only have price extensions shown IF and ONLY IF you are the top result. That is the only position that will show price extensions. That's why these are great to implement into your branded campaigns. Branded campaigns give you the closest thing you will get to a guarantee that you will be the top result.

You can use price extensions in conjunction with other ad extensions except for sitelink extensions.

Price extensions are made up with the following:

- ○ 25-character headline that links to the final URL.
- ✗ 25-character description.
- ○ Price (can be exact price, from price, or up-to price).

There are a few reasons why you should be taking advantage of price extensions:

More Screen Real Estate

Much like other ad extensions, you get more screen space. But, price extensions give you even more space at the top spot which can be the differentiator when a potential customer is searching.

Let's You Showcase Business Offerings in Detail

No other ad extension lets you showcase right in your ad what services you provide quite like a price extension. These jump out to potential customers who are focused on the price for certain services, giving you high quality leads.

Flexible and Customizable

Price extensions allow you to change your extensions based on specific deals you are running. These can quickly be changed without any down time for your campaigns.

Recently Google has expanded price extensions from just mobile and tablet to now include desktop. This means customers can see your price extensions on all devices.

Here is an example from Google of how they appear on desktop versus how they appeared on mobile.

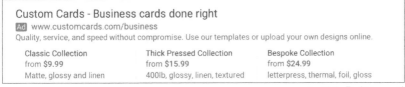

fig. 43-2 : Desktop example

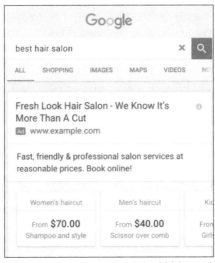

fig. 43-3: Mobile example

Play #43 / Discover The Best Google Ad Extension

Here are a few of the best practices for price extensions if you choose to use them:

Keep Headlines and Descriptions Succinct

Price extensions are susceptible to being cut off with a "…" if your headlines or descriptions are too long. Keeping them short and simple lessens that chance and allows you to optimize that valuable screen real estate.

Select Proper Description

The most common price extension type I use for my clients are "Services" and "Service Categories". Services are specific and use descriptions to explain how a certain type of service works. Service categories have several specific categories that can fall under them.

Update Price Extensions Regularly

Take advantage of how easy it is to update price extensions by using them to highlight seasonal deals or special pricing. It's also important that these extensions match any offers you have in your ad headlines.

Having price extensions across all devices is definitely a bonus to businesses who want to showcase their premier services right on their ad.

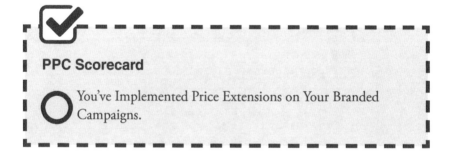

PPC Scorecard

○ You've Implemented Price Extensions on Your Branded Campaigns.

PLAY #44

How To Use Promotion Extensions To Advertise Your Top Selling Products and Services

Play Action:

Implement Promotion Extensions to Boldly Advertise Your Best Deals.

Ever walk through the mall around holiday season and see giant, bold sale signs everywhere? Maybe you're someone who purposely shops around those times because you love a good sale. Now that 76% of U.S consumers shop online, we have to find a way to achieve that giant, bold sale sign effect through digital devices. That's what promotion extensions do.

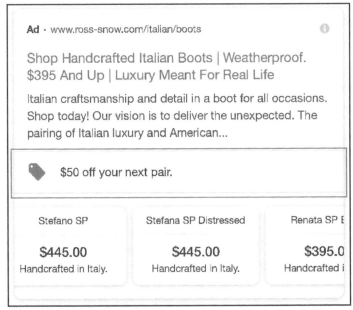

fig. 44-1: Promotion Extension

Promotion extensions highlight a special event of your choosing to let your viewers know about the deals you're running. It's up to you if you choose to include promo codes, a percent discount, or some other offer within your extension. You can create a promotion extension for most holidays and occasions by pulling from a list of pre-populated occasions so you don't have to create new text ads every time. Google really takes the work out of it for you.

This extension will stand out to the prospect's eye. If you're celebrating an occasion or simply offering a deal it will be in bold followed by the details of the sale you're offering. Checkout promotion extension in action. A $50 off promotion for men's italian shoes in *fig. 44-1.*

You can choose to specify what days of the month, day of the week, and time of the day you want to schedule your promotion extensions allowing you to be prepared during those special occasions your clients may expect a sale on services or products.

Promotion extensions are free to add. You'll only be charged for a click on your ad just as you'd normally be charged. More opportunity, same cost.

PPC Scorecard

You've Implemented Promotion Extensions to Highlight a Special Offer.

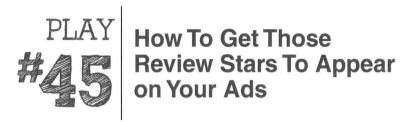

PLAY #45

How To Get Those Review Stars To Appear on Your Ads

Play Action:

Collect Customer Reviews and Meet Google's Minimum Requirements to Show Off Your Positive Reviews.

Seller rating extensions help showcase advertisers with high ratings. They can really help you put your best foot forward when it comes to building trust with your prospects.

They include three features:

1. A rating out of 5 stars.

2. The # of ratings your business has received.

3. A qualifier that explains why you got the rating you did.

What exactly gives you the seller rating that you receive? Google gathers these ratings from a number of reputable business sources that do business reviews in order to have an accurate and well rounded representation of the customer satisfaction level with your business.

If you don't want seller ratings to appear on your search ads you do have the option to remove them, otherwise they are automatic. They will appear without your control and there is no way to set these up. Keep in mind that you're not charged for seller ratings. You are charged when someone clicks on your ad, as is standard PPC practice. It's also worth noting that your seller rating will only show up if you have 100+ unique reviews and a rating of at least 3.5 stars within the last 12 months. Knowing this, it could be worth it to collect positive reviews from your customers in order to stay in the game.

Seller ratings help increase your click-through rate, explain a little more about what you offer, and let your prospects know that you run a reputable business with reviews that speak for themselves. They build trust and will populate automatically if you have the minimum criteria above.

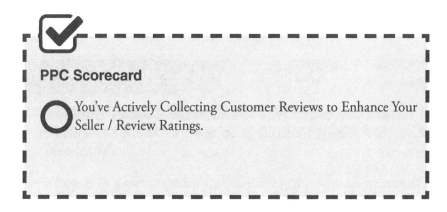

PPC Scorecard

O You've Actively Collecting Customer Reviews to Enhance Your Seller / Review Ratings.

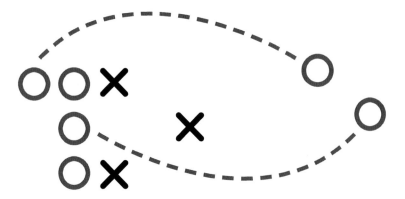

Play #45 / How To Get Those Review Stars To Appear on Your Ads

 PLAY | # Breaking It Down: Get a Behind The Scenes Look At a Top Performing Google Ad

Play Action:

Go Online and Watch The On-Demand Video Walking You Through The Structure of a Top Performing Google Ad.

GO TO: REGISTERPPCBOOK.COM

In this Quick Video You Will Discover:

O   How To Take The Critical Components in the Ad Copy Formula and Apply Them to Your Google Ads.

X   A Step-by-Step Breakdown of Google's Expanded Text Ads.

O   The Most Effective Google Ad Extensions and How to Use Them.

REGISTER NOW

GO TO: REGISTERPPCBOOK.COM

PPC Scorecard

O   You've Watched The Structure of a Top Performing Google Ad Video At **REGISTERPPCBOOK.COM**

"It ain't over 'til it's over."

-Yogi Berra

HALFTIME

GET READY TO CONVERT MORE SALES

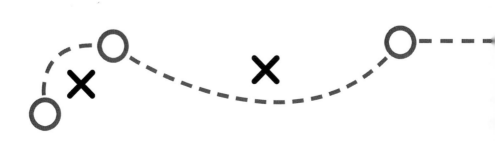

"In baseball and in business, there are three types of people. Those who make it happen, those who watch it happen, and those who wonder what happened."

-Tommy Lasorda

SECTION #5 LANDINGPAGE FUNDAMENTALS

CAPITALIZE ON EVERY CLICK BY SENDING VISITORS TO DEDICATED, OPTIMIZED LANDING PAGES.

You'll Learn What Goes Into A Competition Crushing Landing Page And Why You Need One, How To Rule The Mobile Page Experience, And How To Capture and Convert All Types Of Buyers.

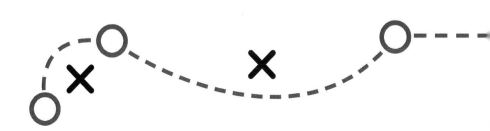

PLAY | **Discover The Importance of Using a Landing Page in Your PPC Campaigns and How They'll Help You Improve Lead Conversion**

Play Action:

Implement Landing Pages in your PPC Strategy and Establish a Conversion Metric by Which You'll Manage Your Account Performance.

Once an interested prospect clicks on your ad, Google has done their job and gets paid. They have delivered a visitor and now it's up to you to take that visitor and enter them into your sales funnel. You do this with landing pages. This is where all the action happens. All too often I see the mistake of businesses who send traffic to the homepage on a website or a webpage that is not relevant to the search intention of the buyer.

> **If you don't use landing pages to support your PPC strategy I would advise against making any investments in PPC. <u>Landing pages do a lot,</u> which you'll discover in this section.**

The goal of a landing page is to control the sales process. Having a dedicated landing page is like having a 24-hour salesperson always on call providing buyers exactly what they are looking for so they enter into your sales process. They answer questions, build trust, provide details, position offers, deliver value and hold the prospect's hand by giving them all the information and comfort they need to pick up the phone and call you.

It's not just smart business- it's a necessity. When it comes to any form of digital advertising, the landing page is the gateway to your sales funnel. It's important to have a dedicated landing page for each unique ad you have so it ties back to the buyer intent.

What does it mean for a landing page to be "dedicated"? Dedicated refers to the page's sole mission of converting leads by creating a personalized experience. Unlike your main website page which serves several purposes like informing clients of your services, describing your business history, location, contact info, etc., your landing page exists to get your customers to buy a specific service or product. Your landing page mimics your ad and points your prospect in a single direction- the path of opening their wallet and calling on you to do business.

You can measure the performance of your landing pages by how well they convert. This is called **lead conversion rate.** This is a simple measurement: the total number of leads divided by the total number of clicks your ads received. This is the single most important metric in all of PPC and is often the hardest to understand.

A strong, healthy conversion rate is the first tell tale sign of how your entire PPC campaign is performing. In fact, when I analyze my client's campaigns this is the first metric I look at because by working to optimize the conversion rate of a given page I can do a few things: **grow traffic, reduce lead costs, and improve lead quality.**

 Steve's PPC Breakdown

Now, I always get the question, "What is an acceptable conversion rate"? The answer to that question is complicated. It really depends on your sales process, how big your ticket is, the average number of days it takes to get a deal done along with many other factors including your budget and how conservative or open you want to run your campaigns.

I can tell you that it's not a perfect score. In fact, having a conversion rate at 90% isn't a sign of a top performing campaign. The higher number means you might be leaving search volume on the table because the campaigns are setup too tight. You show me a PPC account with a 90% conversion and I'll show you missed sales opportunities.

You might only have a handful of keywords you're bidding on that you know convert while leaving other opportunities out there for your competition to grab.

Steve's PPC Breakdown *(continued)*

I would say any conversion greater than 60% means you might have an issue with lead volume. You might have good quality leads at a great price, but there's still <u>a lot more out there you could be going after.</u> At the same time, anything under 6% means you might have a technical issue with your pages, a messaging problem or you're not generating the right traffic.

You want to shoot for somewhere in the middle if your goal is to drive a high volume of leads. If you're happy with a conservative setup only grabbing sporadic leads with a higher conversion rate, then that's perfectly fine as well. Just know that your **conversion rate always ties back to the overall strategy** of an entire account setup.

Let me clarify what I mean with an example: I once worked with a client who worked with one of my competitors. The competitor boasted about their 90% conversion rate. This client complained of low lead volume. Lead cost was not a concern. They wanted more and I knew right away they weren't getting the volume they could so we loosened up the campaign setup, added a stream of new keywords, and doubled lead volume. The conversion rate dropped to around 40% but I was able to double up leads while maintaining costs which had a significant impact on their revenue performance.

It's always a good idea to evaluate how tight or loose your campaigns are being managed. Are you bidding on all the keywords in your market that can result in a lead opportunity? By consistently measuring conversion rate and identifying new keyword opportunities you'll start to grow traffic and control your costs.

You should have a target conversion rate you manage to based on the goals of your PPC account. The best way to come up with a target delta is to go back to Google's forecast engine. See what the maximum budget is that your market can support. If you can support a big budget based on the maximum spend threshold, your conversion rate is going to be on the lower side because the goal of your account is to generate a healthy balance of traffic and leads. If you have a smaller budget, you want to shoot for a much higher conversion rate because you should have a conversative campaign setup.

Keep in mind as you measure lead conversion, you are mostly likely measuring activity in-month. If you have a longer sales cycle you want to look at the numbers quarterly. You may be generating early stage buying activity that does not convert in that given month. When you introduce a followup campaign like remarketing, which we'll discuss up ahead, you'll see your conversion improve in the following months.

If you remember anything from this book, remember this: **Conversion is the most important PPC management metric**. Improving conversion reduces lead cost, improves click-through rates and improves lead quality. There are over 50 numbers and metrics you can look at when evaluating your campaigns. This is the only one to focus on because if you work toward achieving a better conversion outcome- everything else falls into place.

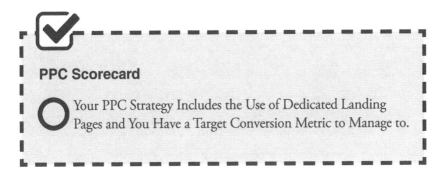

PPC Scorecard

Your PPC Strategy Includes the Use of Dedicated Landing Pages and You Have a Target Conversion Metric to Manage to.

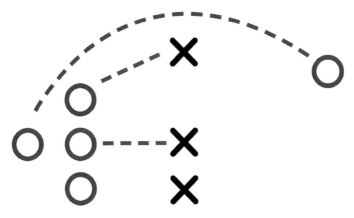

Play #47 / The Importance of Using a Landing Page in Your PPC Campaigns

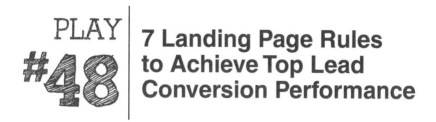

PLAY #48

7 Landing Page Rules to Achieve Top Lead Conversion Performance

Play Action:

Optimize Landing Pages To Get Your Best Possible Lead Conversion Outcome.

True or False: Using landing pages and not your main website will HURT your SEO? This is completely **false**. It's usually some sort of SEO sales guy or Marketing Consultant with no actual experience who will tell you this.

In fact, landing pages do not impact your SEO performance at all. Google does not reward you with improved SEO rankings based on how much you spend or where you send your PPC traffic. Using landing pages actually helps you improve your pay-per-click performance. Remember the goal of the landing page is to control your sales process and is separate from your organic site.

It's always best practice, at a technical level to not index your landing pages to Google's search engine so they do not interfere with your SEO strategy.

I always like to send my traffic to pages off the main site, and for good reason:

- ○ Remember the buyer has a specific need, want, or desire. Providing them with a page that addresses this single thing will improve your conversion rate and overall campaign performance.

- ○ A landing page prevents the visitor from leaving or getting distracted and moving to another place on your website.

O   Using a landing page lets you control the experience, but also identify areas where you can make improvements.

Here are some rules to follow when designing and constructing your landing pages:

1. **Color Selection**- Use no more than 2-3 colors in your landing pages. I've found the color blue to convert the best where black and green convert the worst. Keep the page clean and bright. The colors should be consistent with your brand.

2. **Animations**- When it comes to paid search the rule of thumb is to stay away from animations on your landing pages. This includes video that automatically loads, bouncing gifs, or other elements that might move on the page. If you provide a distraction it will impede the goal of the landing page which is to generate leads. Eliminate distractions for your prospects.

3. **Call to Actions**- When you're first starting out don't have more than 2 call to actions. Your first (and primary) call to action should be your phone number and second, a form. Other call to actions like texting, chat, and direct messaging can be effective, but you don't want to give the buyer too many options without knowing what your baseline conversion metrics are with these two primary components.

   Once you introduce your next call to action, for example a chat feature, you want to see if it helps or hurts your overall conversion. Test, test, test- never accept that something is perfect. If your conversion numbers drop, then eliminate the call to action.

4. **Excessive Plugins**- If you use a platform like Wordpress you'll want to stay away from having excessive plugins. Too many plugins can slow down your landing page performance.

5. **Secured**- This is an important one. You always want to send your prospect to a secured landing page with an SSL certificate. At the time of writing this, there are many browsers including Chrome, Mozilla, and Internet Explorer that will block traffic from coming to your landing page if you do not have an SSL certificate already installed. This means you could potentially be

losing traffic you are paying for right now without it.

6. **Fast**- The last thing anybody wants to do is wait for a landing page to load. You'll need to make sure your landing pages are fast and pass Google's site speed score, especially on mobile.

7. **Naked**- Now don't laugh. This is an actual term used in the internet marketing industry. A "naked" landing page is basically a landing page stripped of all navigation preventing the buyer from leaving to go to another page. Remember the goal of the landing page is to control the sales process and get the buyer to convert. If you give them too many options they may click off the page and the probability of losing them drastically increases.

Following these guidelines will help you create a clean, crisp looking landing page that directs your client through the sales funnel seamlessly.

PPC Scorecard

Your Landing Pages Are Fast, Have a Clean Look and Feel, Are Using Friendly Colors, Are Using Only a Handful of Conversion Elements, Have No Navigation Elements and Are Setup to Prevent Technical Issues.

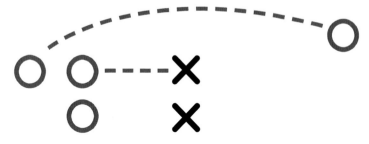

Play #48 / 7 Landing Page Rules to Achieve Top Lead Conversion Performance

PLAY #49

How to Win The Mobile Game and Generate More Smart Phone Leads

Play Action:

Implement Responsive Designed Landing Pages That Work on All Devices to Capture More Mobile Leads.

We now live in a world where almost everyone is walking around with tiny computers right in their pocket. We're plugged in, always connected with access to information at a moment's notice. In fact, we don't even have to type in the information we are looking for anymore we just ask our phones using voice assistants like Siri and Google.

Mobile traffic is the fastest growing segment of all paid traffic. You could say we are in the middle of a *Mobile Revolution* and it's something you want to pay close attention to.

People take their phone with them to figure out the source of their problems. If they have an issue with their heating equipment they may Google *"Heating Contractor"* right in the basement next to their furnace.

If someone notices a shingle has fallen off their roof while going to work in the morning they might Google a roof repair contractor from their driveway. It's more important now than ever that you are setup for mobile success.

Your landing pages should be responsive, adapting the size and style of the page based on the type of device the prospect is searching on. It's now considered "old school" and not a best practice to have a separate page for mobile and a separate page for the desktop experience. Responsive design is key when it comes to your landing pages. It allows you to be consistent across all devices and saves you a lot of time when making edits as well.

Responsive designed landing pages go hand-in-hand with the use of Google's Expanded Text Ads. In the past Google separated the flow of traffic by having dedicated ad formats just for mobile- that is no longer the case. Google's Expanded Text ad format will automatically adjust based on the type of device the searcher is using.

At the same time, there are some mobile elements you want to trigger when the mobile responsive landing page is viewed. In a mobile environment you want your page to deliver a static click to call feature right near the bottom of the screen. See example:

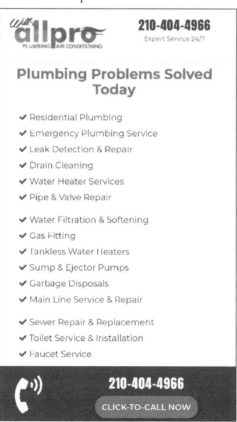

fig. 49-1: Click to call feature on mobile

You want to make it easy for a prospect to click near the bottom of your page by using their thumb to call you. Simple things like making them stretch their fingers to the top of your mobile page might prevent them from taking immediate action.

If you are using forms on your mobile site you want to limit the form fills to no more than just 3 fields and have the form styled for the mobile user making it simple for them to submit it to you. You also want your message (the one from your ad) to carry over and be the first thing they see when they arrive on your landing page.

The more comfortable the mobile experience the higher the conversion rates you will see. Remember some people are lazy, new to technology, or may not be savvy when it comes to having to dig deep to find the information they are looking for so make it an experience that is easy to use and enjoyable for anyone.

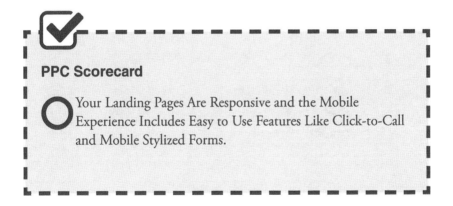

PPC Scorecard

O Your Landing Pages Are Responsive and the Mobile Experience Includes Easy to Use Features Like Click-to-Call and Mobile Stylized Forms.

PLAY #50 | Generate More Leads By Building Landing Pages Designed For the Buyer's Journey

Play Action:

Eliminate Buyer Confusion By Building or Correcting Landing Pages That Are Not Consistent With Your Google Ads.

There are a lot of fast, moving parts to Pay-Per-Click:

- O   The initial search.
- ✕   The ad delivery.
- O   The evaluation of ad copy.
- O   The click.
- ✕   The landing page experience.
- O   The entry point to your sales funnel with a call or form fill.

All these things have to work together in sync within seconds. That's why it's so important your message is clear and consistent on your landing page and matches the message they see on your ad.

Consistency is the key to Google Ads success. Remember your buyer is going on a journey.

If someone searches "oranges" for example, you don't want to send them to a page that shows apples. Your landing page has to deliver consistency at all points of the journey. At the same time you want to make sure all the information communicated matches up to the Ad Copy Formula and is front and center above the landing page fold (that's the part of the landing page before you start scrolling down).

All the Ad Copy Formula elements need to be there:

1. **Introduce the Pain-** What is the customer's problem?

2. **Exploit the Pain-** How does this problem impact their life? Show them.

3. **Solution-** How will your product or service solve this problem?

4. **Benefits-** *"Here's what life will look like for you without the problem."*

5. **Urgency-** Revisit pain, introduce deadlines.

6. **Limited Availability-** Create urgency with an exclusive deal or limited supply.

7. **Call to Action-** Tell the customer exactly what they need to do to get your product.

Everything working smoothly (because of the work you put in beforehand) will help your viewers get from point A to point B without confusion or gaps in the process. Focus on the buyer's intent and you won't fall off track.

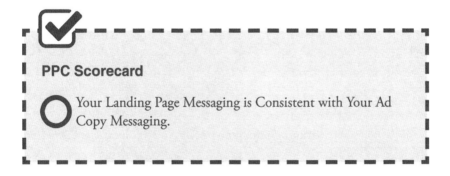

PPC Scorecard

Your Landing Page Messaging is Consistent with Your Ad Copy Messaging.

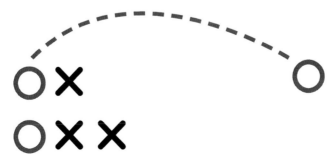

Play #50 / Generate More Leads By Building Landing Pages

7 Essential Engagement Elements of Highly Converting Landing Pages

Play Action:

Incorporate the Right Combination of Text, Imagery, Video and Other Elements to Satisfy the Different Learning Types of Buyers.

What really happens when someone lands on your landing page? They are evaluating your company to see if you are the right fit. They are taking in all of the information. They are learning.

It's important to have the right combination of language, call to actions, graphics, and video on your page to appeal to the different learning styles your various viewers find success with.

What do these learning styles look like?

1. **Visual Learners**- Graphics appeal to this group of people. You want to incorporate pictures of you and your team, pictures of your products and services, pictures of happy customers, and pictures that communicate trust like affiliations, reviews, logos of rewards, and pictures of positive outcomes.

2. **Auditory Learners**- A video or audio element that a user can press to play where you incorporate all of the Ad Copy Formula elements. Reading your offer with footage of your company will satisfy these types of learners.
    Note: It's important if you use embedded video or audio that they load on your landing page from another trusted source i.e. Youtube so as not to weigh down the speed and performance of

your page.

3. **Verbal Learners-** Those who learn through reading and writing. For this group you'll want to incorporate a detailed description of your offer in the form of text on the body of your landing page.

4. **Logical Learners-** These are the learners who are looking for information related to math or science. They are analytical. An argument about return on investment is helpful to appease this learning group.

5. **Social Learners-** Those who learn through the experience of others. They are looking for trust signals, so it's important to include the experiences of other people or references to real reviews on your landing pages.

6. **Physical Learners-** Those who learn by wanting to participate or by doing. If you sell a product or service that includes a visit to a person's home you may have a tangible product with an example of how it works. In other words, something where the person can be hands-on, touch, and feel.

7. **Interpersonal Learners-** These people are mostly concerned with outcomes and may evaluate many options. Here you may consider listing options in your sales copy to prevent them from evaluating other competitors.

By combining several techniques you can be sure to appeal to any future customer that comes your way while keeping your landing page interesting.

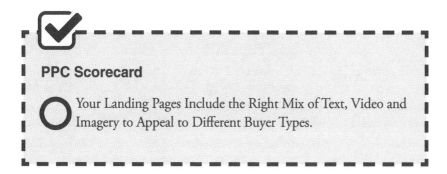

PPC Scorecard

Your Landing Pages Include the Right Mix of Text, Video and Imagery to Appeal to Different Buyer Types.

"Winning is not a sometime thing, it is an all the time thing. You don't do things right once in a while. You do them right all the time."

- Vince Lombardi

SECTION #6
LANDING PAGE
PERFORMANCE
IMPROVEMENT

GET THE MOST OUT OF YOUR LANDING PAGES BY OPTIMIZING THEM FOR PERFORMANCE AND TRACKING SUCCESS.

You'll Learn How To Optimize Your Landing Pages For Speed, Track Each Click, Measure The Success Of Your Keywords, Gather Data About Visitors On Your Pages, Improve Your Landing Page Experience Score, And The Benefits Of Using Different Technologies To Help You Convert More Clicks to Opportunities.

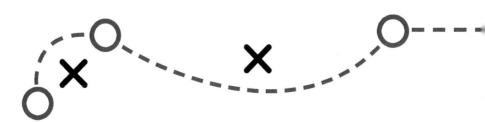

PLAY
#52

6 Ways To Prevent a
Landing Page Disaster

Play Action:

Protect Your Pay-Per-Click Advertising Investment and Power Your Campaigns With The Right Server Setup.

If you're investing any ad spending budget of significance you want to make sure you have the right technical tools in place to get the job done when it comes to your landing page performance. This includes prevention of landing page loading issues and technical disruptions that may be costly to your lead generation performance. Here are some tips on technology that will allow you to sleep easy at night knowing you have the right technical setup in place powering your landing page performance.

#1 Failover DNS

Failover DNS is used to keep a site running in the event of a server or network issue. There's nothing worse than having to pay for traffic that lands on a landing page that doesn't load due to a network or technical server issue. Google won't always catch a landing page that's down in time. With failover DNS software your traffic will move to another IP address that you have running at a different location.

#2 Backup Server

O   In order to successfully run failover DNS you will need a backup server in place at a different location, essentially having 2 servers powering your landing page setup.

○ This might sound like overkill, but if you are making any investments of consequence this can really mitigate any downtime, loss of revenue, or wasted ad spend.

#3 Server Backup

Now if failover DNS backup and 2 servers sounds like overkill, you'll want at minimum a real-time backup of your server so that in the case of a prolonged downtime event you'll be able to fire up a new server manually and get your ads operational.

#4 Downtime Monitor

○ You can invest in a monthly downtime monitoring service that keeps track of your website performance ensuring it's running as expected. In the event of downtime you'll receive an instant notification.

✗ Google won't always catch a landing page that's down, so it's important to have a notification process in place.

○ If Google does catch a down landing page, your ads will be disapproved and you will have to reset/resubmit them for approval.

#5 Dedicated Server

✗ Not all servers are created equal. If you are investing any amount of significance you'll want to have control over your server and how resources are managed.

○ Ensure it's souped up for performance and able to respond quickly.

○ A dedicated server means you own it- not sharing it with someone else. When you share a server with someone else you are sharing resources putting your campaigns at risk if your neighbor decides to do something malicious with their share of the server.

The downside of sharing a server with someone else:

○ If they use the server to spam people with email.

○   If they get hacked you're pages will be at risk, too.

○   If they get a spike in traffic, your site speed can be greatly reduced since you are sharing processing power.

#6 Server Security

It's always a best practice to make sure your server is protected against malware, hacks, DDOS attacks, and brute force attacks (where someone is trying to crack the password into your website with a web security solution). There are a number of services offered out there either 3rd party or included with your hosting provider to help you mitigate these risks.

When it comes to servers, it's best to invest in the right hardware so you don't find yourself in a situation where you're unable to convert traffic you've paid for through Google Ads.

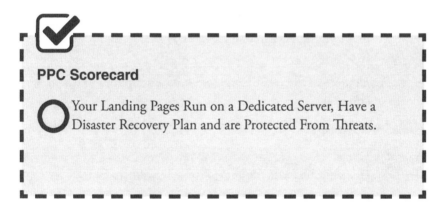

PPC Scorecard

○   Your Landing Pages Run on a Dedicated Server, Have a Disaster Recovery Plan and are Protected From Threats.

PLAY
#53

The Need for Speed: 7 Optimization Tips to Make Your Landing Pages Run Faster and Convert More Leads

Play Action:

Speed up Your Landing Page Performance By Optimizing Media, Minifying Code and By Implementing Page Caching.

Having a landing page that runs smoothly, quickly and efficiently is not just attractive to your prospects, it's crucial to lead conversion.

Research shows that viewers won't wait much longer than 3 seconds for a web page to load before moving on. This could mean lost conversions for you if your page is too slow. So, how do you speed up your page?

Ways to make your landing page run faster:

1. **Optimize your images, video, and other media:**
   As simple as it may sound, resizing your images to the correct size before uploading them can help your page run faster. In general, making sure your media is as concise as possible will go a long way.

2. **Improve caching and hosting solutions:**
   In short, caching is the process of storing data for faster use in a cache. Without any caching at all a user would have to download your page every time they wanted to see your site. Caching will make your pages load super fast. There are different types of caching including page caching, object caching, etc. If you use Wordpress you can use a caching plugin. This will keep your

site running faster by speeding up access to web pages people use frequently.

3. **Run speed audits using Google's page speed tester:**
Running a Google Speed Test is one of the easiest ways to figure out what Google thinks is negatively affecting your page speed. It's a great place to get started if you're not sure why your page is running slow. You'll get a list of recommendations and you can work from there.

4. **Minified or reduced Javascript and CSS:**
Don't worry, this sounds more complicated than it is. Minifying your Javascript, CSS, & HTML is just reducing your code by taking out things you don't need like commas, spaces, and unnecessary characters. Make your code short and sweet for a faster loading landing page.

5. **Implement Google AMP:**
Google AMP, also known as Accelerated Mobile Pages are specifically designed by Google for any publisher to use. Using AMP can speed up your page time by as much as a second. That time matters when three seconds is the most someone will wait.

6. **Invest in a CDN:**
If you still feel like your media is too big after downsizing, you might consider storing your files on an external hosting platform or invest in a CDN. Implementing a CDN allows users to have fast access to your page. Most CDN services will cache your website across a network of data centers and will serve content from the server closest to the searcher. So with a site user from Dallas for instance, they would be receiving data from a server in Dallas.

7. **Use Google's Mobile Speed Score as a Guide:**
Within the Google Ads interface in the landing page section Google will provide you with a mobile speed score (scale 1-10), a mobile friendly click rate, and valid AMP click rate. Using these tools to assess the health of your page speed will give you an idea of where you are now so you can make improvements. *See fig 53-1.*

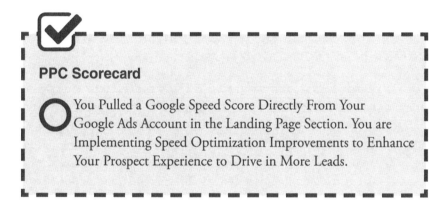

Landing page	Mobile speed score	Mobile-friendly click rate	Valid AMP click rate	Clicks	Imps	CTR	Avg. CPC	Cost
https://acmetools.com/best-sellers View expanded landing pages	4/10	100%	–	41	335	12.24%	$1.93	$79.27
https://acmetools.com/newest-tools View expanded landing pages	9/10	100%	100%	1	34	14.63%	$1.31	$1.31

fig. 53-1: Statistics from GoogleMobile Speed Score

You know that the speed of your page can make or break your user's experience. Get started by optimizing your landing pages today and catch every conversion coming your way.

PPC Scorecard

You Pulled a Google Speed Score Directly From Your Google Ads Account in the Landing Page Section. You are Implementing Speed Optimization Improvements to Enhance Your Prospect Experience to Drive in More Leads.

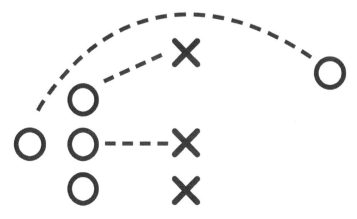

Play #53 / 7 Optimization Tips to Make Your Landing Pages Run Faster

PLAY #54

How You Can Track and Collect The Visitor Details of Every Click

Play Action:

Implement Google ValueTrack Parameters To Collect Key Information About Each Click.

ValueTrack parameters, formerly known as UTM parameters are tags you add to a URL to identify key information coming from Google ads. When your link is clicked on your Google ad, the tags are sent back to Google Ads and Google Analytics through the interaction on your landing pages and you can capture key information. Up ahead I'm going to discuss how you can easily facilitate the capture of this information using call tracking technology.

Google gives you the ability to setup tracking templates at the account, campaign, and ad group level. These templates hinge onto your final URL and deliver key information to help you gain intelligence about your account.

When someone clicks on your ad, you're basically asking Google to give you information about that visitor's session.

Information you can collect from an individual's visit include:

○ The campaign ID.

✕ The adgroup ID.

○ The ad network.

○ The ad creative.

- O   The placement of the ad.
- ✕   The device type.
- O   The model of the device.
- O   The keyword.
- ✕   The keyword match type.
- O   The geographical location.
- O   The ad position.

What does ValueTrack look like in action? After clicking on an ad looking at a Ford F-150, you'll notice in the browser a string of characters in the URL. This string of characters are ValueTrack parameters in action and tie back every click with all of the relevant information you want to collect as an advertiser with Google.

fig. 54-1: Example of a ValueTrack

The above ValueTrack: https://www.ford.com/trucks/f150/2019/?gclid=EAIaIQobChMItPWl9tWf5QIVBOiGCh1dBwBOEAAYASAAEgJgOPD_BwE&searchid=757864944|45440575168|16821271|&ef_id=EAIaIQobChMItPWl9tWf5QIVBOiGCh1dBwBOEAAYASAAEgJgOPD_BwE:G:s&s_kwcid=AL!2519!3!272517223157!e!!g!!ford%20f%20150

The more information you have the more strategic you can be in the future to make data-driven decisions that will impact your conversion rate and cost per lead.

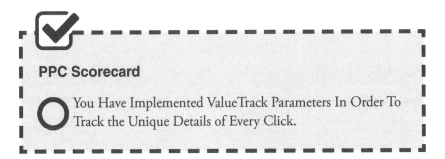

PPC Scorecard

O   You Have Implemented ValueTrack Parameters In Order To Track the Unique Details of Every Click.

PLAY

#55

10 Revealing Pieces of Information You Can Get About Every Visitor By Using Dynamic Call Tracking

Play Action:

Implement Dynamic Keyword-Level Call Tracking to Identify Top Performing Keywords and Critical Visitor Information.

Part of a top performing landing page is what it does for you under the hood. In this case, it's the conversion tracking technology.

You could easily track performance at the campaign level by using a hard coded, static call tracking line. The disadvantage of doing this is not being able to extract all the good information you could be getting with dynamic keyword level call tracking.

There are a number of call tracking solutions out there that automatically assign a dedicated local phone line to each website visitor as soon as they click on your ad. From here they are able to track and collect specific information about the visitor. When the visitor ends up on your landing page they are assigned a tracking line. This tracking line is displayed everywhere a phone number is displayed on your landing page. With dynamic keyword call tracking you are tracking the visitors every move.

Even if a visitor leaves and comes back, that specific line still follows them. This ensures there is no confusion on the part of the buyer because they see a consistent number each time they visit the site. On a deeper level, it provides you with a lot more information.

When setup correctly, dynamic keyword level call tracking takes the visitor information and extracts all the relevant details you want to collect using ValueTrack parameters to help optimize your campaign performance.

The process:

- ○ A visitor lands on your landing page.
- ✗ They are assigned a unique tracking number from a dedicated pool of lines.
- ○ That line is linked to your visitor for as long as they visit your landing pages.
- ○ As soon as they land on the page the visitor is assigned to a unique 'session.'
- ✗ When the visitor calls the phone number it will count as a lead conversion and a conversion is registered with Google telling you exactly which keyword led to the new opportunity.
- ○ The session reveals all the information that led them to the page including:
    - ○ The keyword they typed into Google.
    - ○ The unique click ID from Google.
    - ○ The time of day.
    - ✗ The day of week.
    - ○ The specific ad copy that led them to the page.
    - ○ The specific campaign and ad group within your Google account.
    - ✗ The specific device the user used to find you.
    - ○ The IP address of the visitor.
    - ○ The location of the visitor.
    - ○ The specific cost per click.

All of this information is highly important to the process of understanding what is working and what is not working at the keyword level. It's extremely detailed which gives you more visibility into Google ad performance.

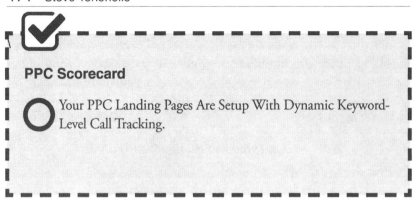

PPC Scorecard

Your PPC Landing Pages Are Setup With Dynamic Keyword-Level Call Tracking.

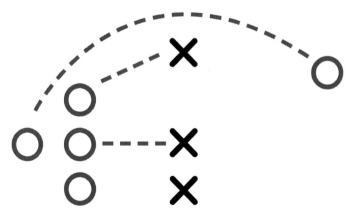

PLAY #56

How To Build Hundreds of Landing Pages in Seconds

Play Action:

Implement Dynamic Landing Pages to Save Time, Improve Your Messaging and Increase Your Conversion Rates.

Instead of creating hundreds of unique landing pages to support each unique Google ad you can implement dynamic landing pages.

Dynamic landing pages give you the ability to easily take text from a Google ad and inject it right on the landing page as soon as someone clicks on your ad. You can display a different and unique message based on specific variables in your ad copy.

As mentioned earlier, it is extremely important that your buyer has a unified and consistent experience from initial search to landing page. Dynamic landing pages allow you to deliver that experience in bulk and will help you increase conversion rates.

I use dynamic landing pages in my own landing page platform, MachinePages. My company, AdMachines, created this platform to make it easy to build similar pages in seconds. They come in handy when I work with a client who services a large volume of zip codes or cities. I could manually develop a landing page for each zip code (which I have pain stakingly done in the past) or I can easily use dynamic landing pages to speed up the process, especially if the offers are consistent across all locations. The visitor who lives in a specific geolocation sees the name of the city along with a local phone line on the landing pages they drop on, appearing **extremely relevant** to the location.

Essentially, a dynamic landing page shows a different and unique message based on which ad is clicked on. At the ad copy level within Google ads, you would setup the dynamic keywords on your final URL that you would like to display on your landing page and this is the trigger point that changes what the visitor ultimately sees.

What I like most about dynamic landing pages is the fact that I can stay nimble and act fast. I can make a change to an offer for a client in minutes rather than taking days to manually adjust every page.

Here's How to Get Started With Dynamic Landing Pages

First you would build a landing page template. The template would require "swap" technology or certain website scripts that automatically change the text based on rules you establish.

For example, when building a large air conditioning repair campaign for one of my clients in Miami, my repair landing page has a headline "Same Day Local AC Repair". My swap technology will change out the word "Local" for the actual city name, ie. "Same Day Miami AC Repair". The swap technology reads the page and makes adjustments to the text in real time.

The landing page will show the relevant keyword to the user based on this information. So if your ad copy read "Local Boston Knee Doctor" you can use the word "Boston" to insert right into the landing page and as your cities change you can inject different city keywords in this example. When a consumer reaches your page, they will see the same city they saw in your ad without you having to develop multiple pages, when someone from Miami clicks on the ad.

Dynamic landing pages save time, offer consistency and makes it much easier to manage your account, especially when it comes to making changes to your offers.

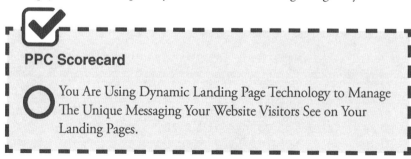

PPC Scorecard

O You Are Using Dynamic Landing Page Technology to Manage The Unique Messaging Your Website Visitors See on Your Landing Pages.

PLAY #57 | **Using Instant Replay Technology to Improve Landing Page Conversion**

Play Action:

Implement Heat Mapping Software to Monitor Landing Page Interaction and Make Improvements to Increase Conversion Rates.

If you've ever wanted to understand how visitors interact with your landing pages now you can with heat mapping software.

Heat mapping software is like having instant replay for your landing pages. It's a conversion rate optimization or CRO technology solution that records and provides you with a playback on how people click, move, and scroll on your landing pages. With visitor recordings you'll be able to see how prospects behave on your page. This helps you identify issues with usability giving you insights into what you can do to make immediate and impactful improvements.

You'll be able to see where prospects drop off the page and where they might get frustrated. Instant Replay will help you figure out what may be contributing to poor landing page performance. With certain solutions you can even see if someone attempted to fill out a form and where they got frustrated and fell off your page.

Steve's PPC Breakdown

Visually reviewing user interaction is something I do often to see if certain elements need to be removed, updated, and enhanced. For example, I have a few window replacement contractors that I work with. I learned after using

Steve's PPC Breakdown *(continued)*

instant replay and studying the film we weren't getting as many form fills as we did after changing the position of the form position. With this information, my team and I moved the form position above the fold and increased the number of form fills which doubled conversions.

Heat mapping technology can also help you identify technical issues on your pages. The most common issues are places where people may get frustrated or where elements look clean to you but look out of position on certain devices or older browsers. You may even identify your page isn't loading on certain browsers. Investing time into learning how your customers interact with your pages can help you create a better experience and increase your conversion rate.

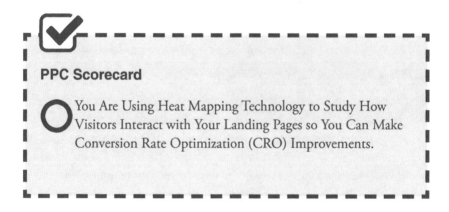

PPC Scorecard

You Are Using Heat Mapping Technology to Study How Visitors Interact with Your Landing Pages so You Can Make Conversion Rate Optimization (CRO) Improvements.

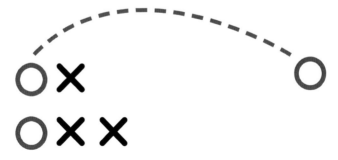

PLAY #58

How To Improve Your Google Landing Page Experience Score and Reduce Your Cost-Per-Click

Play Action:

Identify Your Google Landing Page Experience Score, Make Improvements and Increase Overall Quality Score.

The landing page experience score is one component of your overall Google Quality Score. At the keyword level, Google provides you with a landing page experience score that you can view. It can be *below average*, *average*, or *above average*. In order to see your score, all you have to do is enable it on your column layout. Here's what it looks like:

Conv. rate	Landing page exp. (hist.)	Landing page exp.	Quality Score	Quality Score (hist.)	Clicks	CTR
28.13%	Average	Average	4/10	4/10	32	3.17%
16.13%	Average	Average	5/10	5/10	31	3.04%
30.77%	Above average	Above average	6/10	6/10	13	1.68%
66.67%	Above average	Above average	5/10	5/10	3	0.94%
12.50%	Average	Average	4/10	4/10	8	5.88%
14.29%	Below average	Below average	1/10	1/10	7	2.27%

fig. 58-1: Google Quality Score

This score estimates how relevant and useful your landing page is to the people who click on your ad. It looks to make sure the keyword search term is included on the page and measures how easy it is for people to interact on your page.

At the same time, Google is measuring the mobile speed and mobile interactions of your landing pages and providing separate scores for each.

Working to improve Google landing page experience score will improve your overall keyword quality score. As a result, your overall search impression share will increase and your cost per click will decrease. You'll start to gain more efficiency in these areas if you improve the landing page experience.

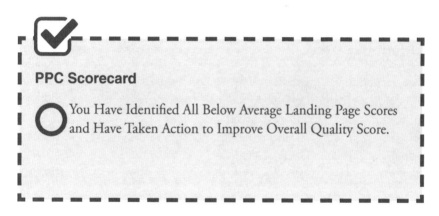

PPC Scorecard

O You Have Identified All Below Average Landing Page Scores and Have Taken Action to Improve Overall Quality Score.

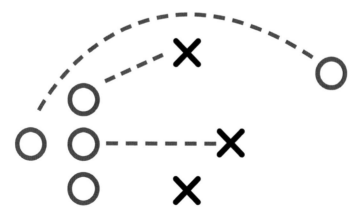

Play #58 / How To Improve Your Google Landing Page Experience Score

PLAY

#59

How To Properly Track and Measure Keyword Conversions

Play Action:

Track Conversions at the Keyword Level of Your Pay-Per-Click Account to Reduce Waste and Control Lead Costs.

One of the biggest technical obstacles most Google advertisers face in lead generation is the ability to measure and track the effectiveness of a given campaign, let alone individual keyword performance.

Earlier, I discussed how you can use keyword level call tracking to track the effectiveness of individual keywords. This is the best way to track conversions because it closes the loop and actually feeds conversion information right back directly into your Google account at the keyword level.

As you can see in the example below, when you have keyword level conversion tracking installed you'll be able to see exactly how many conversions you have generated for each individual keyword. You'll see how many clicks you paid for and how many leads you've generated as a result. You'll also see how much the click traffic cost you along with the individual cost per lead at the keyword level.

This is extremely powerful information because it gives you a batting average for every keyword in your account.

Setting up conversion tracking requires the following:

O   Keyword level dynamic call tracking installed on your landing pages.

○   Automatic tagging setup in Google Ads.

✕   Tracking template setup using ValueTrack parameters.

○   Google Analytics linked to your Google Ads account.

○   Calls and/or form fill goals setup in the conversion actions section in Google Ads.

Once you have all of these parts in place you'll start to see conversions post to your Google account and you'll be able to make decisions impacting the performance of your keywords.

		Keyword	Campaign	Ad group	Status	Max. CPC	Cost	↓ Convers	Cost / conv.	Conv. rate
☐	●	+ac +installation	AC INSTALLATION: SALES FUNNEL	INSTALLATION AC	Eligible	$29.46	$1,003.73	9.00	$111.53	28.13%
☐	●	+ac +install	AC INSTALLATION: SALES FUNNEL	INSTALL AC	Eligible	$29.46	$857.53	5.00	$171.51	16.13%
☐	●	+ac +replace	AC REPLACEMENT: SALES FUNNEL	REPLACE AC	Below first page bid ($30.00)	$29.46	$361.18	4.00	$90.30	30.77%
☐	● ▾	+install +air	AC INSTALLATION: SALES FUNNEL	INSTALL AIR	Eligible	$29.46	$89.10	2.00	$44.55	66.67%
☐	●	+air +conditioner +installation	AC INSTALLATION: SALES FUNNEL	INSTALLATION AIR CONDITIONER	Below first page bid ($32.70)	$17.96	$270.55	1.00	$270.55	12.50%
☐	●	+replace +air	AC REPLACEMENT: SALES FUNNEL	REPLACE AIR	Rarely shown (low Quality Score)	$29.46	$196.92	1.00	$196.92	14.29%
☐	●	+ac +coil	AC TERMS: SALES FUNNEL - WORKING	AC COIL	Eligible	$29.46	$0.00	0.00	$0.00	0.00%
☐	●	+ac +local	AC TERMS: SALES FUNNEL - WORKING	AC LOCAL	Eligible	$29.46	$0.00	0.00	$0.00	0.00%
☐	●	+ac +purchase	AC TERMS: SALES FUNNEL - WORKING	AC PURCHASE	Eligible	$29.46	$0.00	0.00	$0.00	0.00%
☐	●	+ac +purchasing	AC TERMS: SALES FUNNEL - WORKING	AC PURCHASE	Eligible	$29.46	$0.00	0.00	$0.00	0.00%

fig. 59-1

Steve's PPC Breakdown

The Power of Historical Keyword Conversion Performance

Let's say you have a high cost per lead over a $200 delta for example. When you have high lead cost performance you can control it by making the following adjustments to your keywords:

Identify all keywords with clicks and no conversions and reduce your maximum cost per click by 80%. Make sure to perform a keyword maintenance on the all time keyword history.

Identify all keywords with conversions over your delta conversion target cost per lead and reduce the CPC by 50% on these terms.

Steve's PPC Breakdown *(continued)*

Identify all keywords with conversions below your delta conversion target and set the bid rates at a 90-day or 6-month rolling average of the campaign' category CPC. You would choose the window of time that represents a season or entire buying cycle.

By following this method you are eliminating the waste that goes into keyword clicks that do not perform or result in a lead, reducing the lead cost of keywords that do perform over your target delta, and managing your CPC to averages on the keywords that perform so you generate leads at the market rate.

Understanding the inner workings of your campaign will help you further your progress in major ways; get started tracking and measuring today. You'll be able to find your top performing keywords and cut ones that don't serve your account anymore.

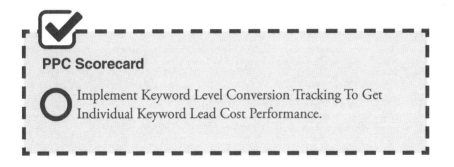

PPC Scorecard

Implement Keyword Level Conversion Tracking To Get Individual Keyword Lead Cost Performance.

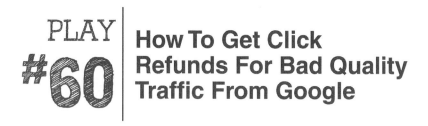

PLAY

#60

How To Get Click Refunds For Bad Quality Traffic From Google

Play Action:

Install an IP Tracking Software Solution on Your Landing Pages to Track Activity and Request Refunds for Malicious Traffic.

Studies have been published stating that 20% of pay-per-click clicks are fraudulent in nature. These can be clicks from bots, clicks from competitors, or even accidental clicks from people who didn't mean to click on your ads.

Google considers this invalid click traffic, which is essentially a click that doesn't come from a real user with genuine interest in doing business with you. These clicks will then be posted as "invalid" meaning they are credited to your account prior to billing so you won't be charged for them. You can see how much invalid click traffic you get right inside of your Google Ads dashboard at the campaign level by adding the "invalid click" column to your keyword dashboard.

Now this system isn't 100% perfect. Bad traffic will still pass through and you will be charged for it. However, Google has come a long way in improving the overall quality of traffic an advertiser receives. They are also much more transparent about invalid clicks by displaying this information direct in your account.

Now, if you can prove clicks are not relevant to your search settings and how your campaigns are configured you can take things a step further by requesting a refund for specific clicks. If there is a discrepancy between what you have been charged and the amount of invalid click credits you received you can hold Google accountable and keep them honest. All you have to do is submit all the substantiating information to Google in order to receive a click refund by filling out a click quality form.

Located Here:
https://support.google.com/google-ads/contact/click_quality

Google will need the following information:

- ○ The date of the suspicious activity.
- ○ The impacted campaigns.
- ○ The ad groups impacted.
- ✗ The specific keywords impacted.
- ○ Summary of your issue.
- ○ IP addresses of visitors.

There are software solutions that automatically do this. In fact, in my company, Admachines, we use our own proprietary software ClickDNA to monitor click fraud and get refunds for our clients.

You can do this on your own by installing an IP tracking solution on your landing pages. An IP tracking solution will tell you how many times a user from a given IP address clicks on your ad.

With this information you can determine if a bot, someone outside your targeted location, or a competitor is continually clicking on your ads in an effort to do harm. Google gives you the ability to block certain IP addresses from ever seeing your ads again, all you have to do is submit it into the IP exclusions setting at the campaign level in your account.

Preventing click fraud is just one more thing you can do to optimize your performance.

PPC Scorecard

○ You Are Identifying Click Fraud and Requesting Click Credits From Google By Tracking IP Addresses on Your Landing Page

PLAY #61 | Benefits of Using Google Analytics and Google Tag Manager on Your Landing Pages

Play Action:

Install Both Google Analytics and Google Tag Manager To Measure, Analyze, and Make Improvements to Your PPC Performance.

Google Analytics and Google Tag Manager (GTM) are two underutilized tools that can be helpful to anyone managing PPC campaigns. They are often overlooked because of confusion. Let's break down what these tools are (in simple terms) and why you should be installing them into your landing pages. Think of this section as 'Google Analytics and Google Tag Manager for Dummies.' Before we dissect these tools let's get some basic terminology down with a short glossary to better understand the tech lingo.

Quick Glossary:

Tags- Snippets of code or tracking pixels from third-party tools.
Triggers- This tells GTM when or how to fire a tag.
Variables- Additional information GTM may need for a tag and trigger to work.

What is Google Tag Manager? *What does it do?*

1. Can help improve your page speed.

2. Consolidate/manage tags, change tags easily.

3. Allows you to work independently of your team or at the same time.

4. Easy to use error checking- has a preview & debug mode.

5. Lets you update your tags for conversion tracking.

6. Lets you test your tags to make sure they load the right page when clicked.

7. Can use triggers to control when your tags fire.

What is Google Analytics? *What does it do?*

1. Helps you understand how users are engaging with your landing page using things like (but not limited to):
   - O **Bounce Rate**- how many users leave your site.
   - ✗ **Time Lag Rate**- which reports the number of days from the 1st interaction to the conversion.
   - O **Audience Report**- breaks down your website traffic by demographic.
   - O **Mobile Performance Report**- Tells you if your site is optimized for mobile performance.

2. Provides information such as: how many people saw your page the day before, what web browser they used, which pages are most popular, etc.

3. Uses machine learning to gain insights from your data.

4. Process and share large amount of data quickly.

Lastly, I'm sure you want to know "Why does this matter to my PPC campaign"? By using Google Tag Manager and Google Analytics you make the system work for you. Google Analytics helps you figure out what you can change right now to get a higher conversion rate. Google Tag Manager allows you to update your tags for conversion tracking, site analytics, and remarketing. See how these advanced tools can help you gain more control over your PPC campaign.

PPC Scorecard

O Google Analytics and Google Tag Manager are Both Setup and Installed on Your Landing Pages

Play #61 / Benefits of Using Google Analytics and Google Tag Manager

Why Bounce Rate Doesn't Matter

Play Action:

Understand Why Conversion is the Key to Your Lead Generation Success.

Over the years I've worked with my fair share of so-called marketing experts or gurus. Or better yet, SEO experts who try to manage PPC accounts. They all talk about bounce rate. I'm not sure why, because if your goal is to generate leads your primary management metrics are conversion and lead quality.

What is more important to you, a higher conversion rate or a lower bounce rate? It really depends on your goals. When it comes to lead generation you want a high conversion rate and bounce rate doesn't really matter. People tend to throw the term "bounce rate" around but have no clue what it means.

By definition (from Google) a bounce is a single-page session on your site. In Google Analytics, a bounce is calculated specifically as a session that triggers only a single request to the analytics server. For example, when a user opens a single page on your site and then exits without triggering any other requests during that session.

This means if a visitor goes to your landing page, gets your phone number without going to any other pages, picks up the phone, and calls you (then becoming a lead and a new sales opportunity) they are still considered a bounce because they didn't navigate to another page. They got what they needed- your contact information which resulted in a conversion.

This is why bounce rate does not measure the success and performance of a landing page. Unless you are running a complicated campaign requiring many steps, bounce rate doesn't matter. Conversion and lead quality are the key components to the overall health and well being of your campaigns.

If someone is giving you advice about your bounce rate- run.

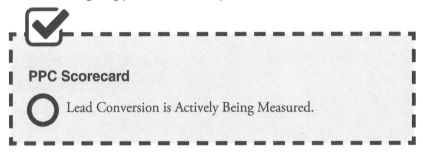

PPC Scorecard

Lead Conversion is Actively Being Measured.

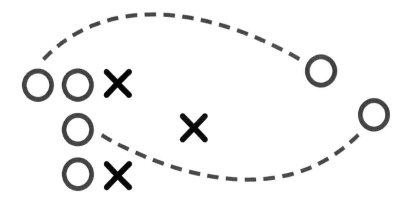

"It isn't the mountains ahead to climb that wear you out; it's the pebble in your shoe."

\- Muhammad Ali

SECTION #7 CAMPAIGN TYPES

GET THE MOST OUT OF YOUR PPC EFFORTS BY TAKING ADVANTAGE OF DIFFERENT CAMPAIGNS AND AUDIENCE TARGETING FEATURES ON GOOGLE AND BEYOND.

You'll Learn How To Recapture Prospects With Remarketing, Protect Your Brand, Harness The Power Of The Microsoft Advertising Network, Target Facebook's Massive User Base, And Get Above Traditional Search Ads With Google Local Service Ads.

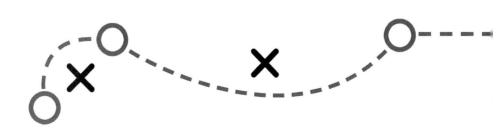

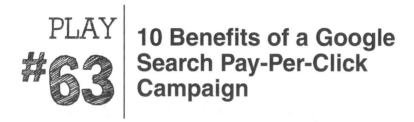

PLAY

#**63**

10 Benefits of a Google Search Pay-Per-Click Campaign

Play Action:

Get Started with a Google Search Campaign and Take Full Advantage of What Google Pay-Per-Click Advertising Has to Offer.

This book is heavily rooted in one pay-per-click campaign- Google Search. It's the one area where my company, AdMachines manages more than $10M in ad spend each year, generating upwards of 25,000 leads per month. I have been working with Google Ads since 2002, the same year Google introduced the ad solution. I've seen it all with close to 20 years managing paid search campaigns and have personally helped hundreds of local businesses make Google pay-per-click advertising work for them.

Keep in mind, the whole spirit of pay-per-click advertising is to pay for a click after consuming the benefit of someone seeing your ad and clicking on it. It's pay-as-you-go advertising, you should never pay upfront for it and you always want to access your account and pay Google direct. You can stop and go with no minimum ad spend. There are no contracts. You just need to signup and open an account.

Some of the Many Advantages to Google Search Campaigns:

1. Ads no longer look like ads- they easily blend in to the page. The only indicator now is that it will say 'ad' in small writing next to the URL.

2. Ads are now larger and allow more space for headlines and descriptions, giving advertisers more room to display their

message. You can custom create as many ads as you want and Google will help you test your ads so you're getting the best possible response rates.

3. Ad extensions can help you boost your response rates even more.

4. Search campaigns target the active user based on their search intent, (the keyword they type into Google) so they're highly effective for generating leads when you can match their keyword to your product or service offering.

5. Whether advertising to a city or an entire region you can control the location of your ad so you're always targeting the right consumer.

6. You have the ability to use timing to your advantage- only advertising at the times you want.

7. You can control the device where your ad appears, so if you identify most of your customers search from a mobile device you can allocate your budget to this area.

8. You can control your lead quality by implementing negative keywords and using broad match modified keywords. Both of these tools will prevent bad traffic from entering your sales funnel.

9. You can target specific demographics like never before. If you're looking for a certain age group, gender, or even homeowner status you can find it.

10. You can control your costs. Google gives you the ability to track keyword performance, set your own bid rates, establish a budget and make changes at any time. You can also set Google up to manage your performance based on a fixed cost per lead.

Google has come a long way since 2002 and things are only getting more exciting. There is no other advertising vehicle available to local businesses that offers immediate performance and transparency. Take full advantage of all the benefits a Google Search Campaign now offers. Use all of the available features to control your outcome.

PPC Scorecard

You've Setup a Google Search Advertising Account.

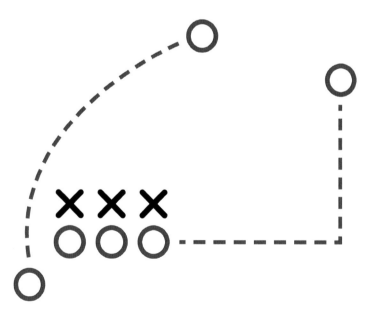

Play #63 / 10 Benefits of a Google Search Pay-Per-Click Campaign

PLAY #64 | Pay-Per-Lead With a Google Display Campaign

Play Action:

Implement a Google Display Campaign and Generate Leads Using the Cost Per Acquisition Model.

There's a good chance if you get your news from FoxNews, CNN or MSNBC, get your weather from weather.com or watch sports on ESPN.com you will see an ad that runs on the Google Display Network.

Unlike Google search campaigns where a searcher types a keyword into Google and you pay for a click, a Display Campaign runs on a network of publisher sites where you can set it up so you only pay for performance.

Benefits of a Google Display Campaign:

O   Your ads can be placed on the sites you choose, targeting the specific audience you want.

O   They help promote brand awareness and gives you the ability to run promotions to a group of people within a targeted geography.

X   Huge reach- the Global Display Network reaches over 2 million sites.

O   Google makes it easy to launch a campaign without hiring a designer to put together banner ads. Google will do most of the work for you by uploading your text, images, logos, and other information. Google then uses machine learning to generate responsive ads and only shows the ones with the best performance history.

○   Plus, Google has recently made it possible for advertisers to run display ads using a Cost-Per- Acquisition (CPA) model. This means you only pay for the leads your campaigns generate. It's pay-per-conversion advertising. The Google Display Network is very appealing as a complimentary strategy to run alongside your Google Search campaigns.

Get started using Google Display ads now and grow your brand, keep your company top of mind on the sites you want, and generate leads on a cost per lead basis.

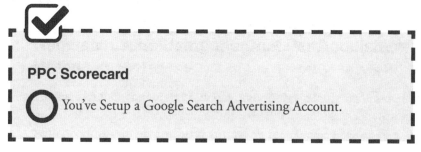

PPC Scorecard

○ You've Setup a Google Search Advertising Account.

Generate More Leads with Remarketing

Play Action:

Implement a Google Display Remarketing Campaign and Bring Prospective Buyers Back to Your Sales Funnel.

Prospective buyers are clicking on your pay-per-click ads. You're getting plenty of traffic, but that traffic is not converting to leads. On average 80 percent of web-users say they have visited a website before they were ready to make a purchase. Maybe they had to talk it over with their significant other, or just needed more time to think about it, or they just forgot. Whatever the reason, they've clicked on your ad but did not taken action.

When you try to sell a high-ticket item, you are naturally going to have a longer buying cycle. Throughout that buying cycle prospects are going to evaluate their options and consider alternatives. In a perfect world, everyone would buy from you instantaneously. Unfortunately, that's not the case and buyers can be unpredictable. The best defense you can put in place is a system to automatically follow-up with hot prospects and increase your probability of sales success. So, how can you protect your advertising investments by keeping your prospective customers engaged and your local brand top of mind?

You can start a meaningful, value-building conversation with **remarketing.**

When a prospect clicks on one of your ads and lands on your website you can enter that visitor into an automatic follow-up campaign using Google's powerful remarketing technology. Remarketing on the Google Display

Network takes those people who left your site and adds them to a list. Then when they are on ESPN, Weather.com CNN, Fox News, MSNBC or another site they'll see your ad and will be reminded to complete whatever unfinished business they had on your site- whether that means making a call, filling out a form, or take the first step in making a purchase.

Think of remarketing as an *insurance policy* for the money you put into your online advertising budget. You got people to click on your ad and you paid for that click. You want to do everything in your power to turn those clicks into **paying customers**.

Now is the perfect time to invest in remarketing campaigns because Google has made it easier than ever before. Remarketing has become smarter. Google now follows your web visitors on every device they use including mobile and desktop when a prospective buyer is logged into Google Chrome. This is new for Google and the technology has evolved in recent years. Google once used cookies which were limited to the visits based on the device- not necessarily tied to the user. The new way goes into much greater depth with demographic information on the types of people who click on your ads.

One thing you need to keep in mind before you set up a remarketing campaign is that you will need a minimum of 100 people on your remarketing list before your ad will show up on the Google Display Network.

 Steve's PPC Breakdown

Here are two unconventional ways you can tie a remarketing strategy into something you are doing already.

Email:

Doing an email blast to your existing customer and prospect list will get your remarketing campaign activated fast. You need 100 people to click on your email and visit your landing page. The landing page is the trigger point for a remarketing campaign and it should contain the proper Google remarketing code. This is what Google uses to place the website visitor into

Steve's PPC Breakdown *(continued)*

a remarketing campaign list. Ads will start to follow your visitors wherever they go on the internet once they hit the landing page. Email is a great way to activate the campaign so it's primed to support your other campaigns.

Offline Marketing

Typically there is a shelf life with traditional marketing. If you make investments in direct mail, print, radio or TV you can keep your message alive much longer by implementing a remarketing effort on Google. When you integrate your offline advertising with remarketing you can keep your message alive and turn a one and done campaign into a campaign that lasts for the complete duration of a buying cycle. With Google remarketing you can serve ads to people who respond to your marketing for up to 540 days.

All you have to do is purchase a vanity domain to support your given offline campaign. Prospects are driven to a landing page that matches the offline message. This is a great way to extend the life of a campaign because once someone types in the URL, they will be automatically added to a remarketing list and will begin to see your ads.

Developing Your Remarketing Strategy

Once you commit to launching a remarketing campaign you want to figure out the best strategy. The great part about remarketing is you can be very specific to different audiences on your list. I'm going to give you a few examples on how you can actually use remarketing to its full potential.

Cross Promote

I work with a lot of multi-trade home service companies. Companies that provide heating, cooling, plumbing, drain cleaning and electrical services. A lot of these services have really quick sales cycles- often less than 24 hours.

For example, if a prospect lands on an emergency plumbing landing page and calls for service immediately it wouldn't be a good fit to sell additional plumbing services because it's likely the searcher already took action. However, we can use remarketing to cross-sell a different service or product within the business. Perhaps this company also services heating systems. An offer to perform a heating system maintenance or tune-up would be a great cross sell to create interest with this already engaged audience.

Upsell

What did you leave on the table in your last sale? You can use remarketing to upsell. The more offers you create and place in front of the customers who already know, like, trust your business, the more opportunities you give yourself to generate additional revenue.

If you have ever booked a flight you may start to see remarketing ads for rental cars. If you own car insurance you may have seen remarketing ads for home insurance from your provider. Every day companies you do business with are trying to upsell you with remarketing ads and you can do the same.

Answer Sales Objections

Right now as you read this you have a list of prospects interested in potentially doing business with you. You already answered their sales questions and they are in the decision making process, they just haven't pulled the trigger on making a purchase. You can use remarketing to address their most common concerns or obstacles they face, preventing them from moving forward in a sale.

If prospects are not moving forward due to financial reasons you could build a remarketing campaign that offers a financing plan. If the reason they are not purchasing is due to timing you could launch a remarketing campaign that offers an incentive with a hard deadline. The goal of these campaigns is to help you accelerate buying cycles and tackle objections you may not have uncovered or addressed in the initial sales presentation.

Top of Mind Brand Awareness and Referrals

Use remarketing to stay in front of your existing customers and build long term relationships. Keep them coming back to you by promoting your brand, promoting your employees, by communicating your good deeds in the community, showing off recent work and showcasing other customer experiences and reviews. At the same time you can ask your customers to refer business to you by developing a referral program.

Remarketing is a powerful communication vehicle that will help up drive in additional sales. Just remember, when someone clicks on your ad the sales process begins and you have an opportunity to remind people to come back and take action. Remarketing will do this. It will also help you reduce your overall cost per lead. Since someone already clicked on your ad and you paid a premium, remarketing can inexpensively bring them back to your sales funnel and have them take the next step in the buying cycle. It's the ultimate online way to protect sales opportunities.

Up ahead I'm going to discuss other ways and advertising channels you can use to launch remarketing campaigns.

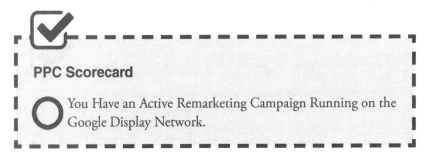

PPC Scorecard

You Have an Active Remarketing Campaign Running on the Google Display Network.

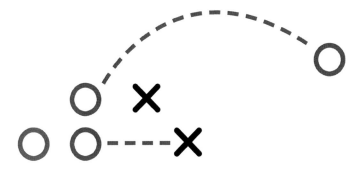

Play #65 / Generate More Leads with Remarketing

PLAY #66 | **How RLSA Ads Will Help You Reduce Your Cost Per Lead**

Play Action:

Implement RLSA Ads to Recapture Opportunities and Reduce Lead Costs.

Let's say you have someone interested in your product or service. They find you on Google and click on your ad. Then they get busy and about a week later they come back to Google and pick up their search again. They start over. This time, instead of displaying the same ad, you can call out the fact they already expressed an interest in your company by customizing your ad to the returning visitor. This is a remarketing ad on the search network in action, all made possible by Remarketing Lists for Search Ads or RLSA.

Remarketing Lists for Search Ads (RLSAs) are a smart way to target a very specific group of people: those who have already visited your website. Traditional remarketing ads and RLSA ads both use cookies to track users who have already visited your site in order to continue to advertise to them.

Unlike traditional remarketing on the display network which shows visitors a banner ad, RSLAs give you the ability to serve your text search ad to past visitors on good old fashioned Google Search.

This is an effective campaign to launch because it gets your ad back in front of engaged prospects and helps you protect yout initial click investment. When they go back to search on your keywords again your ad will be clear, present, and often you can recapture the prospect at much lower bid rate than you did the first time around. This will help you reduce your cost per lead because initial clicks are rebounding back your way.

After regaining the attention of these prospects you have the opportunity to use what you know about where they dropped off in the sales process to offer a discount, serve them an ad that's more tailored to their needs, and give them an overall better offer than what they saw the first time around.

For example, if the history is showing you that the majority of your prospects tend to leave after putting your product in their cart, an ad offering 10% off might help persuade them to stay and purchase. If you own a service company and the majority of people going to your site are looking for emergency type services, the RLSA ad you serve needs to talk about speed, reliability, and efficiency.

RLSA ads are a must have for anyone running search ads.

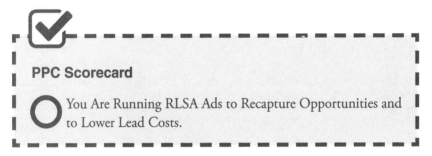

PPC Scorecard

You Are Running RLSA Ads to Recapture Opportunities and to Lower Lead Costs.

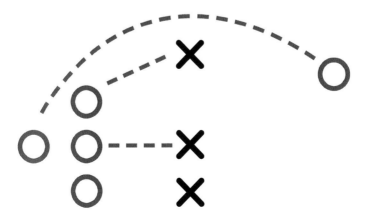

Play #66 / How RLSA Ads Will Help You Reduce Your Cost Per Lead

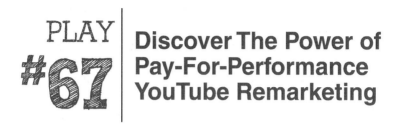

PLAY #67 | **Discover The Power of Pay-For-Performance YouTube Remarketing**

Play Action:

Implement YouTube Trueview Ads to Bring Past Website Visitors Back to Your Sales Funnel on a Pay-Per-View Model.

Fact: By the time you finish reading this play more than 300 hours of video will have been uploaded to YouTube. YouTube is an extremely powerful place to run video ads and recapture opportunities. More and more people are going to YouTube as they cut the cord on traditional cable service.

YouTube remarketing works in a similar way to the traditional remarketing campaigns I discussed earlier. You make a video, setup a youtube campaign right in your Google Ads account, link your remarketing audience to it and away you go. Now, there are a number of video campaign types you can run. I'm going to break them down for you:

○ **Trueview In-Stream Ads-** This is the most popular and effective ad format you'll see on YouTube. They are a skippable video that appears before the main video. I recommend a video no more than 30 seconds. The benefit of trueview ads is you only pay for a complete view or when someone interacts with the video by clicking on a link.

○ **Bumper Ads-** These are short 6 second videos that work extremely well on mobile. As it relates to remarketing, this is the perfect ad to remind someone to come back and take action on your landing pages.

○ **Trueview Discovery Ads-** These are the ads you see in the YouTube search results, basically ads to show your videos and drive customers to your channel.

Below you'll see an example of metrics you'll pull from YouTube. Unlike traditional PPC where you are billed for clicks, YouTube allows you to bid on a CPM basis, which is essentially a cost you set for every 1,000 impressions you want. You can see in the example that I'm setup with a Trueview ad, so I'm only paying for actual views, and in this example is less than 20 cents per completed view or interaction.

fig. 67-1 : Trueview ad

The goal of YouTube remarketing is to drive action to an already engaged audience- the people who already clicked on your search ad and visited your landing pages. This is the best way to dip your toe in the water and get started with YouTube advertising. I am only scratching the surface here with the power of YouTube. At a bare minimum you want to implement remarketing campaigns to reengage your audience to bring them back to your sales funnel.

☑

PPC Scorecard

○ You Are Running YouTube Remarketing TrueView Pay-Per-View Ads.

PLAY #68 | Protect Your Goodwill With a Branded Campaign

Play Action:

Implement a Branded Search Campaign to Protect Your Goodwill, Capture Interested Buyers, and Reinforce Your Messaging.

Branded campaigns are advertising campaigns you can run on the Google Search and Display Networks. You are essentially setting up a campaign bidding on your business name terms. You can customize your ads to include key information about your business, promote your current offers and showcase your reviews.

You've probably heard the old saying, *"your best offense is your best defense."* Branded campaigns work to protect your goodwill in the marketplace and are often very inexpensive to run.

Even if you already show up organically in the first position for your brand name, it's always a best practice to bid on your brand terms in an advertising campaign. Because if you don't- your competition will. Plus it gives you an opportunity to really dominate the search engine results page for your brand.

A competitor bidding on your name means they'll show up in the search when someone types in your name. If you're not bidding on your own name, your competitor might be taking traffic away from you. In Google's eyes this is perfectly acceptable as long as they don't confuse buyers by using your business name in their ad copy.

In my experience, competitors who decide to take branded traffic away from you aren't really generating quality leads. They might get lucky here and there, however most buyers who search for you have the intent in doing business with you. It will be hard to sell that prospect on hiring another company when they've searched for you. Nevertheless, it is always a good idea to protect your brand and give your loyal buyers a clear and easy way to contact you.

Branded campaigns are also smart to implement to support other marketing campaigns. If you advertise on TV, radio, print or direct mail a percentage of people who respond to these campaigns and express an interest will generally type in your business name into Google. They are looking for your company information or are exploring your offer in further detail. It's important to support your major offline campaigns, making sure your PPC ads are consistent with the message.

Running a branded campaign is a smart practice that will help you protect your goodwill, protect your brand from losing opportunities, and will reinforce your message and capture traffic from other marketing sources.

PPC Scorecard

O   You Are Running a Branded PPC Campaign.

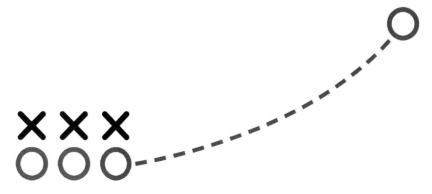

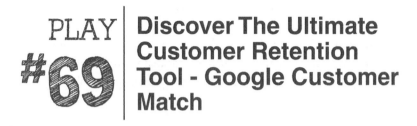

Discover The Ultimate Customer Retention Tool - Google Customer Match

Play Action:

Implement Google Customer Match and Stay Connected with Your Existing Customers on Google Search, Gmail, YouTube and Display.

Google Customer Match is an advertising tool that lets you use your offline and online data to reach and engage with your existing customers all across Google Search, Gmail, YouTube and Display.

You essentially upload a data file of customer contact information, create a campaign targeting this Customer Match audience and the people assigned to this campaign will start to see your ads.

> **It's Google's first time targeting people based on identity.**

It's an exciting opportunity for you to gain more conversions and increase the lifetime value of your existing customer relationships. Unlike Facebook which requires either a mobile phone number or email address, Google is able to identify your customers using many data points including name and mailing address information.

At the same time, once you upload your customer list Google creates a digital ideal customer profile using their Similar Audiences tool. You can then expand your list to include people who share similar characteristics of your existing customers.

Customer Match is an excellent way to remind customers to come back to you for a routine service, to purchase a new product or to upsell an item associated with a recent purchase. If your business depends on an existing customer base to generate sales then Customer Match is the perfect tool to implement in your paid search strategy.

One of the many benefits of Customer Match is the ability to manipulate your bidding strategy in a given campaign. You can put a rope around your customers and ensure if they are out there searching for something you offer, you'll be positioned to snag the opportunity or at least be in the conversation. All too often business owners are so focused on generating new customers they neglect the opportunities sitting right in front of them in their customer database.

 Steve's PPC Breakdown

Now keep in mind, you only want to use Google Customer Match if you own your PPC account or trust your Manager. Otherwise, once you hand over your data to a 3rd party provider there is no guarantee your list won't end up in the hands of one of your competitors in the future. This is especially important if you work with a provider that doesn't allow you to access your account information or if you don't pay Google direct.

Take advantage of Google Customer Match to increase your prospects' brand loyalty, promote repeat purchases, and keep your current custoemrs engaged.

PPC Scorecard

O You Are Running a Google Customer Match Campaign to Generate Repeat Sales From Your Existing Customers.

PLAY #70 | How To Target the People in Your Market Ready to Buy Using Google's In-Market Audiences

Play Action:

Implement Google's In-Market Audiences and Target the People in Your Market Who Have Exhibited Buying Signals.

You can now reach potential customers while they are actively researching, kicking tires or comparing the types of products or services you sell with Google's In-Market Audience Targeting. This targeting feature gives you the ability to get in front of and connect with people in your market who are most interested in what you have to offer based on their search behavior, history, and intentions.

With In-Market audiences you can disrupt your competition's sales pipeline by inserting your business into the buying conversation, even if a prospect hasn't clicked on your ads.

In-Market audience targeting uses machine learning to predict a consumers' intent. It helps advertisers like yourself reach consumers at the optimal time as they are comparing products and just about to make a purchase.

Current activity and recent browser history are both used to determine in-market audiences. Knowing your audience has used services like yours in the past or purchased similar products to what you sell increases the likelihood that they'll convert. Machine learning takes a lot of the guessing out of the advertising process and automatically targets these hot buyers. Using in-market audiences is like having a crystal ball- giving you the ability to pinpoint and target people in your market who are going to buy.

There's a good chance Google has an in-market list for your type of business. They continue to add more detailed lists as time goes on. Let's say you are a home improvement contractor selling window replacements. Google has an in-market audience called "door and window installation" you can target in your market. If you own a GMC dealership you can target people shopping for GMC trucks, Chevy trucks and even people who are in the market searching for an auto loan.

It's a smart idea to consider all of the pathways to purchase. In the home improvement example above I could also target homeowners in the market shopping to refinance their mortgage or looking for a home equity line of credit.

You can narrow the in-market audience down even further by demographic information including targeting homeowners who are men and/or women in a given age group.

Targeting has come a long way with Google. If you haven't tried experimenting with it and you are a bit gun shy about making a pay-per-click investment, this is a great place to start. You have absolute control over the audience you serve ads to with this option. Starting here will really restrict who will see and engage with your ad. By selecting the appropriate audience, you can put probability in your favor for achieving top conversion performance. If you just want to run a conservative campaign and just your ads to people who have exhibited strong buying signals you can do that with in-market audiences.

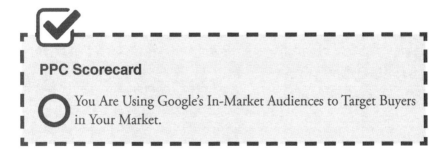

PPC Scorecard

You Are Using Google's In-Market Audiences to Target Buyers in Your Market.

 **PLAY** | **Microsoft Advertising Network: Run Pay-Per-Click Ads on Bing, Yahoo & AOL and Generate Low Cost Leads**

Play Action:

Launch a Microsoft Advertising Campaign on Bing, Yahoo and AOL and generate low cost leads.

There's gold available for mining on the Microsoft Advertising Network. Formerly known as just Bing, the Microsoft Advertising Network now includes three primary search engines: Bing, Yahoo, and AOL.

Here are some stats:

- O   Microsoft claims that their audience spends 35% more online when shopping compared to the average internet searcher.
- O   There are 5.5 billion unique desktop searches per month on these networks.
- X   45% of the users are over the age of 45.

There are fewer users on the Microsoft search network compared to Google, which is expected considering Google is the world's largest search engine. But here's the good news. There's less competition and costs are lower to acquire leads on the Microsoft Ads network. If having two ad platforms concerns you, then you can rest at ease. Microsoft Ads function similar to a Google Ads auction; in fact they are so similar in terms of the advertising product, Microsoft has a tool to extract your Google campaigns so you can easily set them up on Bing.

With Microsoft Ads you have more control at the campaign level. You can target just Bing and Yahoo, just search partners, or both. Whereas with

Google you can only target Google search or Google search and partners. When it comes to demographic targeting, Google and Microsoft Ads are similar in that you have a huge amount of control in who you choose to target with your ads. The one interesting advantage Microsoft has over Google is that it owns LinkedIn and is starting to integrate LinkedIn information into Bing campaigns.

Summary of Microsoft Ads Benefits:

- ○ 36.2% of U.S desktops search on Bing. Not using Bing ads could mean omitting about a third of your client base including older adults, which tends to be the majority on Bing.

- ○ Average cost per click tends to be almost **half** of a Google Adwords click cost.

- ✕ People prefer Bing for image related searches, so if your ads are image based you may consider Bing over Adwords. First think about what you're selling & the nature of your ads.

- ○ You can estimate your cost per click using the Bing Ads preview tool.

Steve's PPC Breakdown

Oftentimes I get the question, *"Should I invest on Bing and if so when?"*. I'm personally not a big fan of launching a Microsoft campaign right away, especially when working with a new client. I like to run my Google Ads for a few months, tighten them up, get a healthy cost per lead along with a fully optimized campaign that is delivering quality leads. When I feel like my Google campaigns are locked and loaded, that's when I like to fire up Microsoft.

It's pretty straight forward. I use a tool provided by Microsoft to extract and essentially clone my Google campaigns. I always reduce my bid rates on Bing by about 75% and run Bing ultra conservatively. Bing is a great equalizer. What I mean is if my lead costs are let's say $50 each on Google and I can generate Bing leads for $20, Bing will help me reduce my overall cost per lead across all advertising platforms. Bing helps me look good with my clients.

Steve's PPC Breakdown *(continued)*

At the same time, after listening to hundreds of recorded phone calls from leads generated by Microsoft, I can tell you with 100% confidence that Bing delivers an older demographic- mainly baby boomers. Unless of course you live in Seattle (where Microsoft is headquartered)- that's a totally different animal!

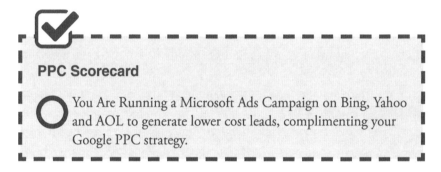

PPC Scorecard

You Are Running a Microsoft Ads Campaign on Bing, Yahoo and AOL to generate lower cost leads, complimenting your Google PPC strategy.

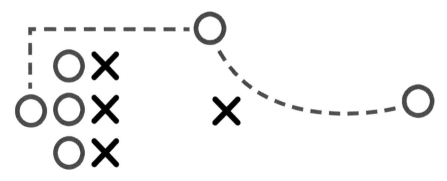

PLAY **#72**

Generate Leads with Facebook Using 2-Step Marketing

Play Action:

Understand How-to Effectively Generate Leads on Facebook Using 2-Step Marketing.

Facebook has over 2.41 billion active users. Clearly, it is a marketing hotspot for anyone looking to reach a large pool of prospective buyers.

Much like the other advertising platforms we discussed, Facebook has the capability to target specific audiences based on demographics, location, interests, and even behaviors. This helps assure you your message is getting in front of the right people since lead quality is always more important than quantity in advertising.

Facebook is actually a lot tougher to advertise on because it is interruption based marketing. With Google, your website visitor generally types in a keyword and you pair that keyword up with a matching ad. They are actively looking for your services and are receptive to the ads. Facebook actually requires a little bit more infrastructure. I call what I'm about to explain to you 2-Step Marketing.

With Facebook people are looking at conversations from their family and friends, looking at pictures and funny videos. It's a fun place. A place of entertainment. A place of enjoyment. Your advertising has to be entertaining, engaging and fun to fit in here. You first have to create an interest. Usually this is a piece of content that engages the audience. They click on your content in the various ad formats to read, watch, or interact with it and in that content you sell your product or service. That's the second step- your call to action.

Here's an example:

A local water softener company wants to sell a whole home water softening system. These systems can range in price from $4000 and upwards so I'd consider it a big ticket item. The company could easily run an ad on Facebook offering homeowners who meet your target requirements a "Free In-Home Estimate."

Alternatively you can run an ad using content "7 Signs You Need a Water Softener." In the body of the content you'll discuss why the buyer's skin might be dry, why their clothes are fading and why they might see calcium build up in the sink or shower. You can develop content that hits the buyer at an emotional level. Throughout the content you talk about how your company solves these problems and you offer a Free In-Home Estimate as your call to action. This is 2-Step Marketing and it is the most effective way to advertise on Facebook to a cold audience.

The vast variety of ad styles available to choose from certainly sweetens how you can put this content into action.

What type of Ads does Facebook offer?

- O **Photo Ads**- Lets you boost an existing photo from your FB page.

- O **Video Ads**- Shows your team and/or product in action with video content.

- X **Carousel Ads**- Lets you use up to 10 photos or videos to show your product(s). You can even create 1 panorama photo.

- O **Slideshow Ads**- Short video ad from a collection of still photos or video clips.

- O **Collection Ads**- Only for mobile devices. Showcase a product customers can click to buy without having to leave Facebook.

- X **Instant Experience Ads**- A full screen ad format that loads 15 seconds faster than a mobile website outside of Facebook.

- X **Lead Ads**- Only available for mobile devices. Designed to make it easy for people to give you their contact information without a lot of typing. You can see where these might come in handy.

O   **Dynamic Ads-** Allows you to promote targeted product ads to the customers who are most likely to buy them. Reminds a potential customer to complete their purchase.

O   **Messenger Ads-** Photo, video, carousel, and dynamic ads can all be set to appear in Facebook messenger. 1.3 billion people use messenger every month so this is prime territory. You can also run "click-to-messenger" ads that feature a call to action button that opens a messenger conversation with your Facebook page.

O   **Facebook Retargeting-** Gives you the ability to put any one of these ad formats in front of the people who visited your website.

X   **Facebook Audiences-** Gives you the ability to import your customer list and target these customers using any of the above ad formats.

O   **Facebook Look-a-Like Audience-** Here Facebook can create a look-a-like audience of website visitors or existing customers helping you expand your reach of potential customers in your market.

 Steve's PPC Breakdown

Even if you do not plan on advertising on Facebook in the near future, I highly recommend that you setup a Facebook advertising account and install a Facebook Pixel on your landing page and website. The Pixel will collect information and allow you to easily launch campaigns when you're ready to get started with Facebook.

If you are just starting out with Facebook, the best and most effective campaign to launch right away would be a retargeting campaign, reminding those people who may have clicked on your Google Ad to come back to your landing pages and take action when they are surfing on Facebook.

If you've been looking to expand your marketing outside of Google or Microsoft, Facebook is the next frontier. Users are on their Facebook accounts each day, so why not serve them an ad where they are spending their free time already with 2-Step Marketing.

PPC Scorecard

You Have Installed a Facebook Pixel on Your Landing Pages and Website.

Play #72 / Generate Leads with Facebook Using 2-Step Marketing

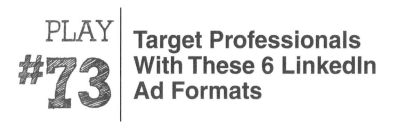

PLAY | **Target Professionals With These 6 LinkedIn Ad Formats**

#**73**

Play Action:

Understand The LinkedIn Advertising Formats.

The biggest advantage of LinkedIn ads is the LinkedIn audience: people of the business world. It's a fact that LinkedIn is home to every sort of profession from the service industry to the medical industry and so much more.

LinkedIn, realizing the opportunity they had to reach serious advertisers, has been working to make it a more effective platform to do so. LinkedIn (owned by Microsoft) now allows you to create ads based on your goals.

Your goal should one (or more) of the following to use LinkedIn Ads:

O   Brand awareness   O   Lead generation

O   Website visits   O   Website conversions

✗   Engagement   O   Job Applications

O   Video views   O   Retargeting

So you have your goal- now you'll be able to choose from 6 types of LinkedIn ads:

1. **Sponsored Content**- You promote an article or post from your company page.

2. **Direct Sponsored Content**- Placed directly in the users news feed to lead to higher engagement levels. You can use text and

larger images to attract the eye.

3. **Sponsored InMail**- These ads need to come from a personal LinkedIn, not a branded page so consumers don't feel like they're being spammed or sold something. They feel more like they're communicating with a representative of the business rather than being served an ad.

4. **Text Ads**- Small ads that appear on the right rail of the LinkedIn feed or beneath the "people you may know" section. The quality of your text is vital here for starting a conversation.

5. **Video Ads**- Promote your videos to a targeted audience.

6. **Lead Gen Forms**- Can be used with Sponsored Content and Sponsored InMail. The user doesn't have to leave LinkedIn to fill out a form.

Once you've set up your LinkedIn ads you'll want to pay close attention to the performance. LinkedIn lets you do this by looking into social actions (LinkedIn members who are interacting with your content) and adjusting budget.

 Steve's PPC Breakdown

Even if you do not plan on participating with LinkedIn Advertising I would advise you set up an advertising account. Next, install the LinkedIn tracking script on your landing pages and website so you can start to collect data about your website visitors as it relates to Linkedin. You want this avenue to be primed and ready if you ever decide to launch ads there.

PPC Scorecard

⭕ You Have Installed the LinkedIn Tracking Script on Your Landing Pages and Website.

PLAY #74 | Dominate the Local Advertising Market By Launching Google Local Search Ads

Play Action:

Become the Premiere Local Service Provider by Starting Local Search Ads to Capture Leads at a Lower Cost.

You have amazing reviews on Google, your star rating is high, and you want to make sure the customers closest to your business find you fast. There's no better way to accomplish this than signing up for Local Service Ads.

Google Local Service Ads (LSAs) are a global solution to local needs. In fact, they account for 13.8% of search engine results pages clicks. These ads are specifically tailored towards Home Service Professionals like HVAC Companies, Heating Contractors, Plumbers, Electricians, etc. but their reach is ever expanding. Most importantly, there's no cost to sign up and the lead cost tends to be lower than traditional Google Search Ads. These ads serve the customers looking for a trusted local home service provider. I find these are a great way to get into online advertising if you've been nervous to commit in the past. Let's explore the world of LSAs in the section below.

How do Google Local Service Ads Work?

When a potential customer searches for a service they'll see local, eligible professionals listed above the paid search ads. Local Service Ads will show:

- O A business number.
- ✗ Hours.
- O Ratings.
- O And reviews.

It's every piece of information a potential customer would want to when looking for a home service company quickly. You can see LSAs on desktop, tablet, and mobile searches. Look at the example below:

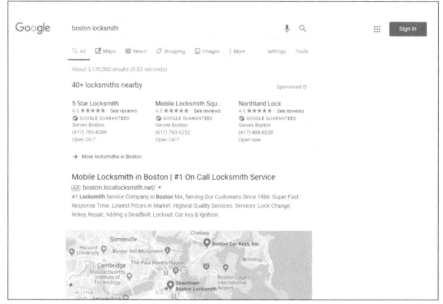

fig. 74-1: Local Service Ads

You'll notice each business has a green checkmark with the phrase "Google Guaranteed". This is the key to local service ads and why Google pushes them above other paid search ads. This Google Guarantee proves to customers that your team has earned Google's stamp of approval as a reputable business. Google Guarantee also protects customers with a lifetime cap for coverage of $2,000 with jobs booked through Local Service Ads.

Why should you care about this check mark?

If you have this check it means that:

- ⭕ Your technicians have passed a background check by a third party Google Provider.
- ⭕ You've met licensing requirements.
- ✖ You are obligated to notify the background check company of any new employees or legal issues.

○ You cannot use the Google guaranteed badge outside of Google Local Services.

Getting guaranteed by Google can take a few weeks since they do background checks through a third party service, but once completed your customers will know a trusted professional is coming to their home. But what makes them different than search ads besides a green check mark? Why should you look into this campaign type?

How Are They Different Than Search Ads?

LSAs are not the traditional text ad that you may be familiar with. Google pulls most of the information from a profile you set up at the beginning of this process along with your Google My Business. You're not writing ads or sending prospects to service specific landing pages, which can actually be a drawback to this product. There's no landing page experience to build trust or entice longer sales cycle buyers.

Even though Local Service Ads are a paid ad type, rankings are incredibly important to their success. When space is limited like it is in this case (only 3 businesses can show at a time), you'll need a higher ranking to ensure your ads are appearing.

Keep in mind that with LSAs your ad's rank is considered based on different factors than the quality score including:

○ How close you are to potential customer's locations.

○ Your review score/# of reviews you recieve.

✗ Your level of responsiveness to people who contact you.

○ Your business hours.

✗ If they've received serious or repeated complaints about your business.

When it comes to cost, LSAs are essentially pay-per-lead. You're only charged when a prospect interacts with your business by placing a phone call or filling out a form. With Google AdWords you set a daily budget which must be managed daily in order to keep it in check. With LSAs, you set the weekly budget and Google will only spend up to what you allow. The typical lead cost on LSAs is just under $30 per lead, but this can vary depending on service type. Make sure you have a budget that can accommodate at least 20 leads/week or else your competition will grab this traffic.

But How Do You Know You'll Get Qualified Leads from LSAs?

When a prospect clicks on your Local Service Ad, Google will ask them to confirm the job and service area. If you're a match, the prospect will see all of your information (qualifications, ratings, reviews…) before giving you a call. If you're not in that person's area, Google will save you the trouble and cost of connecting with them. When you set up your profile, Google will ask for your service area and services you offer.

 Steve's PPC Breakdown

You now know all about Google Service Ads and you think they might be just the right tool to help you grow your business, but you don't know where to start. Checkout the step by step guide below and get your Ads working for you today.

1. **Check your Eligibility:**
   Are Google Local Service Ads available in your location? Local Service Ads are found all across the country and there are plans to expand so this most likely won't be a challenge for you no matter where you live.
   Just go to: https://ads.google.com/local-services-ads/.

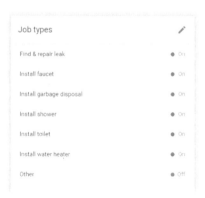

fig. 74-2: Google Service Ad options

Steve's PPC Breakdown *(continued)*

2. **Create your Business Profile:**

   Your profile is very important because it will be used to figure out who matches with your business. You can edit: your weekly budget, your business hours, your service areas, and your job types. You can also add highlights if you choose such as, "Voted Best In Service 5 Years in a Row." You'll fill out this information in your sign up form. Much like online dating, you'll want to be as honest as possible to attract the right people. Never say your team can do a job that isn't actually under the umbrella of work you're qualified for as I mentioned above.

3. **Submit your License and Insurance:**

   In order to be qualified to earn the Google Guarantee you must first prove that you are in fact a licensed professional. Keeping your paperwork current is vital.

4. **Pinkerton Background Check:**

   Because the nature of home service jobs tends to involve entering someone's home, car, office, or other personal setting Google works to ensure customer safety by having all advertisers undergo a background check with Pinkerton. The great news is...it's free!

Final Tips:

- ⭘ Don't forget to check back as Google offers updates to this service.

- ✗ Remember that Local Service Ads are their own product and run independently of Google Ads and Google My Business, budget included. A Google Ads campaign can run at the same time as a Local Service Ad, but it doesn't have to.

- ⭘ You don't have to manage any keywords. You simply have to select your service category and job types and Google will choose appropriate keywords for your ad.

- ✗ As stated earlier, responding quickly and aiming for 5 star service will take you a long way.

Play #74 / Dominate the Local Advertising Market

○ **Stay on top of your budget** as it will directly impact your leads in this situation since you're charged per lead. Try to budget for at least 20 leads per week.

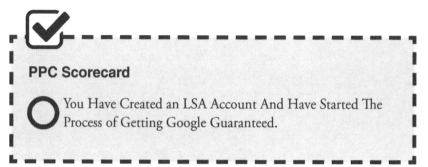

PPC Scorecard

○ You Have Created an LSA Account And Have Started The Process of Getting Google Guaranteed.

"Champions keep playing until they get it right."

— Billie Jean King

"Winners never quit and quitters never win."

- Vince Lombardi

7ᵀᴴ INNING STRETCH

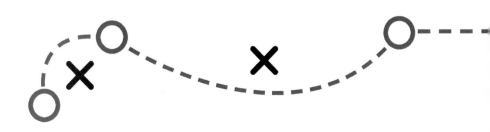

*"I never worry about the problem.
I worry about the solution."*

- Shaquille O'Neal

SECTION #8
PAY-PER-CLICK
PERFORMANCE
MANAGEMENT

CONTROL YOUR OUTCOME USING GOOGLE'S TARGETING TOOLS. FOCUS ON LOCATIONS, KEYWORDS, AND DEVICES THAT PRODUCE YOUR BEST LEADS AND CUT THE DEAD WEIGHT.

You'll Learn How To Target Your Best Zip Codes, Utilize Google's Campaign Schedules, Eliminate Poor Traffic With Negative Keywords And Location Exclusions, Increase Qualified Traffic From Your Best Performing Devices, And Balance Your Budget To Get The Best Return On Investment.

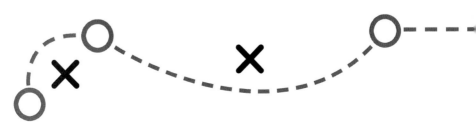

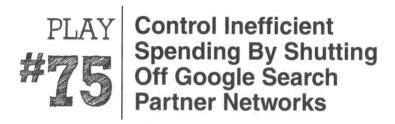

PLAY #75 | Control Inefficient Spending By Shutting Off Google Search Partner Networks

Play Action:

Shut Off the Google Search Partner Network in Your Campaign Settings to Avoid Budget Bleeding.

The default campaign setting when launching a campaign for the first time is for Google to automatically include your campaign in both traditional Google Search as well as the entire Google Search Partner Network. The search network includes more than 500,000 sites, directories, and other search engines.

Traditional Google search happens on Google.com, the Google Play Store, Google shopping, Google Maps, and the Google Maps app. Google Search Partners include sites like Amazon.com, YouTube, The New York Times, and many others. This is an extended network of places where your ad can appear.

It's my personal best practice to contain and limit my clients' exposure on the Google Search Partner Network. I have found that budget bleeds much faster, there is a lot of inefficient spending and limited results on the Google Search Partner network. The Partner Network does not give you the ability to target or control where your ads appear like traditional Google Search.

In your campaign settings turn off search partners by de-selecting the checkbox in the network section. This quick fix can save you a lot of frustration and will give you greater control over your performance.

If you decide you might be thinking about turning on search partners because you want to capture more traffic, there are many more places for you to get qualified traffic first. I'd recommend exploring the Microsoft Ad Network which has Bing and Yahoo, and Facebook advertising first.

fig. 75-1: Campaign settings

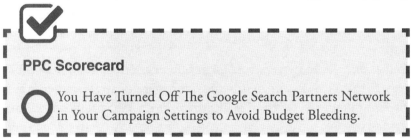

PPC Scorecard

○ You Have Turned Off The Google Search Partners Network in Your Campaign Settings to Avoid Budget Bleeding.

PLAY # **Control Lead Generation Volume and Costs By Using Ad Timing to Your Advantage**

Play Action:

See How Your Campaigns Perform By Time of Day and Make Adjustments to Your Ad Scheduling to Control Lead Costs and Volume.

"In the right place at the right time." - (idiomatic) At a location where something good is about to happen at just the time of its occurrence; lucky; fortunate; able to obtain a benefit due to circumstances.

You're going to find when you pay close attention to your pay-per-click strategy that Google is cyclic. There are patterns that happen throughout the year, throughout the seasons, on certain days of the week and at certain times of day. With Google's scheduling feature you can control when your ad appears by time of day and day of the week in order to take advantage of these timing nuances in your business.

This is extremely impactful to your ad's relevance because it gives you the ability to create campaigns based on customer needs at specific times of day. Let's say you offer windshield repair services. You could run your ad from the time you open, let's say 7am through 12pm and your ad copy can say, *"Call before noon to get your windshield replaced today!"* At noon you can cycle in a new campaign for *"next day windshield replacement."* This is where you can use speed and timing to your advantage.

Google gives you the power, control, and flexibility to run your ads and ensure that they're relevant at any given time offering you a higher probability of success.

Steve's PPC Breakdown

In the keyword section of your campaigns you can create a performance report that will show you how many conversions you've generated by time of day in a given time frame. You can get this information for the entire account or you can break it down by campaign.

This report will show you the actual lead costs on the hour. It's a really powerful report that measures how competitive your market is at different times. It also shows you the pockets of time where search volume is the highest. This one report can help you calibrate your spending and align it to the times where you see the most volume.

Keep in mind Google Ads is a real time auction and a game of supply and demand. Both you and your competitors are fighting for exposure. When volume is low, costs are going to be high. When there is more than enough volume, costs will be lower. In my experience, competitors beat each other up during the slowest times and exhaust their budget, meaning they aren't in the game when it matters the most- during the rushes when your market is the busiest.

When you have Google setup correctly and you're tracking conversions you're able to see how many leads you generate in a given hour. You can analyze the information to see exactly what you're paying by time of day. You can also see at what percentage you're performing.

How can you use this information to make adjustments to the timing of your ads? If you identify an underperforming time of day, you can eliminate this time from running ads and put more budget in the times that produce the best result.

At the same time you can run the same report by day of the week to analyze which days are delivering your best leads at the most efficient cost. Keep in mind you want to make sure you are analyzing data over a full business cycle and have plenty of knowledge when you make these types of decisions ie. over the course of a month, quarter or year. Don't make a snap decision based on just a few days.

Another consideration, as it relates to your competition, is time. You'll want to pay close attention to when your competitors are coming in and out of the Google auction and when they are displaying ads. If their ads are not showing later in the day then there's a good chance they don't have enough budget to support their current setup or not enough capacity to handle the lead volume.

Knowing this information is like having the golden ticket when it comes to your goal of generating the most leads at the lowest cost. In this instance, you can time your ads for later in the day to generate leads at a discount because it's really you and your competition that set the price when it comes to bidding and the overall cost per lead.

At the same time, you want to pay close attention to the last week or so of the month. You'll notice some of your competitors falling off the map. That's because they've exhausted their budget. This gives you the opportunity to have a really strong end to your month by making adjustments to your timing strategy to achieve optimal lead generation performance toward the later part of the month.

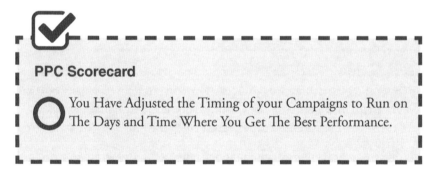

PPC Scorecard

You Have Adjusted the Timing of your Campaigns to Run on The Days and Time Where You Get The Best Performance.

Play #76 / Control Lead Generation Volume and Costs By Using Ad Timing

PLAY #77

Control The Locations Where Your Ad Appears To Enhance Lead Quality, Reduce Overhead & Achieve Better Revenue Performance

Play Action:

Build Out Your Campaigns at a Hyper Local Zip Code Level and Control How and Where Your Ads Appear. Get a Read on The Competitive Landscape of Each Market & Implement a Location Strategy to Control Your Return on Ad Spend.

With Google you can control the areas where your ads appear. Most advertisers make the mistake of blanketing their ads in a large area and trying to be everywhere using only one campaign.

I like to use Google's geolocation controls to my advantage and build out ads that resonate with the local area I'm targeting. I do this by:

- O Working the name of the city or town into my ad.
- X Using a local phone number in my ad.
- O Driving people to the landing page with the city name in it.

I build campaigns for each zip code or city I want to target instead of piling all of the zip codes into one campaign. Building out campaigns for each city takes much longer, but the benefits are well worth it. Using these techniques will help you appear to be the local go-to expert, will help you control lead quality and give you the flexibility to control bidding, budget management, and messaging at a hyper local level. This is all done in an effort to control lead quality and lead costs.

With Google you can target people based on their city or zip code in the location settings. At the same time, you can restrict specific areas and prevent people in a given area from seeing your ads. These exclusions can be just as important as what you include in your targeting, especially if you want to block telemarketers from other states clicking on your ad and calling you to sell something. Another example is that perhaps you own a business in New Jersey close to New York City but you don't service there. Blocking searches from NYC will prevent people from mistakenly searching for your business and driving up your click costs.

What's interesting is when you build hyper local campaigns you'll get greater detailed information about the competitive landscape in a given zip code. You'll be able to see with an auction insights report a complete breakdown of all the competing advertisers in a specific location. At the same time, you can see exactly how much search impression share you own at the zip code level and how often your ad appears in the top spot compared to everyone else. When you run a single campaign with all of your zip codes included in it you don't get this detailed level of competitive information.

Next is cost by location. When I build campaigns at a local level I can compare the costs of the campaigns seeing exactly how each city or zip code is performing compared to the rest. This will show me specifics on what my lead costs are by zip code.

I like to routinely ask my clients for a revenue performance report by zip code or average transaction value by zip code and cross reference it to how much I am spending in a given area. With this information I can invest more of the budget in the areas that generate the best result. Why continue to make investments in the areas where you don't generate an acceptable rate of return on your ad spend?

If you identify you're spending a lot of budget in one area but not getting the return you were hoping for, you can use this information to cut the location entirely or reduce the budget and apply it to the other areas.

At the same time, if you run the type of business where you travel to someones location you now have the flexibility to turn campaigns on and off at the zip code level. So when you get busy, instead of shutting down your whole operation, you can shut down campaigns in the areas you know you can't service due to capacity. This prevents you from investing in leads you can't service.

It's always a great idea to control your lead costs, but have you considered the overhead you pay in fuel, wages and inefficiencies in servicing that opportunity? What if you could spend a little bit more on your leads and significantly control your overhead by focusing your budget around a desired location? With a big enough territory you can accomplish this by using Google's geotargeting controls to your advantage.

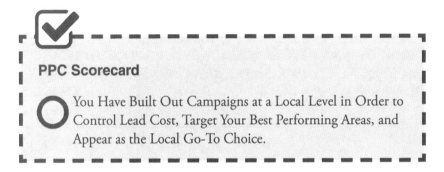

PPC Scorecard

You Have Built Out Campaigns at a Local Level in Order to Control Lead Cost, Target Your Best Performing Areas, and Appear as the Local Go-To Choice.

PLAY #78 | Control The Cost of Clicks Resulting in Competitor Confusion

Play Action:

Block Unwanted Calls From People Who Are Looking For Your Competition and Eliminate Bad Quality Traffic.

Have you ever run into a situation in the past where you mistakenly received a phone call from a prospective customer looking for one of your competitors? It happens more often than you think.

A small minority of my clients want these calls. The majority consider them a nuisance because they are frequently huge time wasters and can eat away at your budget. Others would argue that buyers aren't loyal and that there is a small probability of converting the customer over to them. Of all the calls I've listened to, and after countless years of managing both of these types of strategies, I can tell you with 100% confidence that there is an extremely low probability of success in converting a loyal customer who searched for a competitor using their branded name. Your budget is better invested in real client acquisition.

Here's how to prevent this traffic from coming into your call center:

O   First, you want to look up all of your competitors in the local market. Do this by going to Google maps. Search for the products and services you offer in each of the cities where you want to run ads. You'll get a complete list of providers this way.

X   Next you want to scrub through this list and delete the terms you plan to bid on. For example, let's say you own a local electrical business. You identify your competitors to be "*Bob's Electrical*," "*Jim The Electrician*," and "*Ethical Electricians*." Based on this list you would delete electrical, electrician and electricians. These are good terms for your business. Your final list would include "*Bob's*," "*Jim the*," "*ethical*."

○ Take these remaining terms and create a negative keyword list in Google Ads in the library section.

○ Going to the keywords section in your account find the negative keywords list and apply them to your campaigns.

✗ You will no longer receive calls from people searching for your competitors and if you do, you will be credited with an invalid click or will the opportunity to receive a click refund.

Steve's PPC Breakdown

At the same time, you might find a competitor attempting to take advantage of your goodwill by bidding on your business name and injecting the name of your business in their ad copy. You can prevent this from happening by obtaining a federal trademark registration for your brand. You can submit your trademark registration to Google and they will enter it into their database. The competitor will no longer be able to serve ads on Google with an active federal trademark using your business name.

The best way to protect your brand and control the flow of traffic is to launch a branded campaign where you bid on your own company name, securing the top spot and protecting all the traffic searching for you. If you make any sort of investments outside of Google PPC like TV, radio, or direct mail this is a great way to ensure that people looking for you get to the right spot.

PPC Scorecard

○ You Have Implemented a Competitor's Negative Keyword List to Prevent Bad Quality Traffic From Clicking on Your Ads.

PLAY

#**79**

Control Who Sees Your Ads & Improve Lead Quality With Powerful Targeting Features

Play Action:

Implement Custom Targeting Controls in Your Campaigns to Enhance Lead Quality.

Google has come a long way in terms of targeting. In the past, there was no real way to filter or narrow down the audience you wanted to target. Now there is an array of options you can use to gain control over the audience you appear in front of. By implementing Google's targeting features you'll be well on your way in improving your overall lead quality.

In addition to targeting your audience by time of day, by location, and by keyword you can filter who can see your ads in the following ways:

- O **Demographics**: Target your ads based on how well your products and services trend with users in certain locations, ages, genders, and device types. You can easily find this right at the account level or within the campaign section in your Google Ads account.

- X **By Affinity**: Advertisers with TV campaigns can extend a campaign online and reach an audience using Google Search or the Display Network. You can target people who have an affinity interest in "Home and Garden" for example.

- O **In-Market**: Show ads to users who have been searching for products and services like yours. These users may be looking to make a purchase or have previously made a purchase and could still be interested enough to interact with your ads.

○ **Custom Intent**: Choose words or phrases related to the people that are most likely to engage with your site and make purchases by using "custom intent audiences." In addition to keywords, custom intent audience's lets you add URLs for websites, apps, or YouTube content related to your audience's interests.

✕ **Similar Audiences:** Expand your audience by targeting users with interests related to the users in your remarketing lists. These users aren't searching for your products or services directly, but their related interests may lead them to interacting with your ads based on your current customer base.

○ **Remarketing**: Target users that have already interacted with your ads, website, or app so that they'll see your ads more often. These users can be in any stage of conversion, as long as they've visited your site or clicked on your ad before. These users may even return to complete a purchase.

✕ **Audience Targeting**: One of the newest and most exciting enhancements to audience targeting is the introduction of detailed demographics and in-market audiences. Within the audience section in a given campaign you have the ability to target, observe and exclude certain lists from a library within the Google's audience controls.
For example: If you sell air conditioner repair you probably don't want a phone call from someone who rents their home. You can now exclude renters from seeing your ads. At the same time, if you are a bank looking to sell more mortgage solutions you can target homeowners in the market searching for home equity lines of credit. An auto dealership may also want to consider targeting people who are searching for an auto loan. There are a number of smart lists you can target by.

○ **Customer Lists**: You can import your very own customer lists and Google will help you identify customers who use Google as a search engine using Google Customer Match. Unlike Facebook where you need to have a mobile phone number or email address, Google will accept first name, last name, and address information. Getting your customer information into Google makes sense, especially if you want to create campaigns specific to your existing customers.

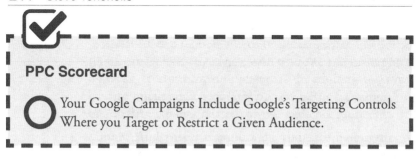

PPC Scorecard

Your Google Campaigns Include Google's Targeting Controls Where you Target or Restrict a Given Audience.

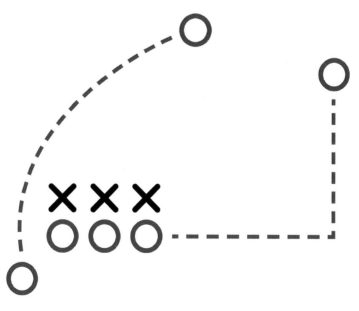

Play #79 / Control Who Sees Your Ads & Improve Lead Quality

PLAY

#80

Control Bad Quality Traffic Eating Away At Your Budget

Play Action:

Brainstorming Exercise! Develop a List of Negative Keywords to Deflect Bad Quality Traffic That Can Bleed Your Budget.

You have the power to control the quality of traffic that views, clicks and interacts with your ad by implementing a list of negative keywords.

We already talked a little about negative keywords in an earlier section. Here, we're going to delve deeper into how to identify and brainstorm negative keywords to protect your investment. Negative keywords will deflect bad quality traffic- essentially the traffic that's not relevant to your campaigns. It's always best practice to have more negative keywords than keywords you are actively bidding on.

Consider the search intent of the person searching Google and block the categories and situations that do not make sense to you. By thinking like a searcher, you can block keywords you don't want to trigger your ads, and easily add them to your negative keywords library.

fig. 80-1: Negative library

In this example we're going to take a look at your local window replacement contractor:

The Paths Searchers Take

The Do-It-Yourselfer:
This person may type in...

- ○ How to replace a window
- ✗ Do-it-yourself window replacement
- ○ Window replacement directions
- ✗ Window replacement tools
- ○ Insulation for replacing windows

In this example the phrases "*how to*," "*do-it-yourself*," "*directions*," "*tools*," and "*insulation*" should be added to your negative keyword list to prevent this type of traffic.

The Off Topic Search:

These are the search terms that will trigger your ad if you do not already have them in place for the general term '*windows*':

- ○ 1998 Toyota Corolla rear view window replacement
- ✗ Dollhouse windows
- ○ Microsoft Windows for dell computer

There are three opportunities to block traffic here in the Toyota example:

- ○ A list of all car manufacturers ie. Toyota, Honda, GMC, Ford, etc.
- ✗ A list of all auto models ie. Camry, Civic, F150, Tahoe, etc.
- ○ A general list of years 1998, 1999, 1990, etc.

There's a good chance your window replacement company doesn't replace dollhouse, car windows, or deal with computers. You'll want to think of situations where the keyword may bring in off-topic search. You can see how quickly off topic search can bleed your budget and the importance of building a large list of negative keywords.

Closely Related Search Terms:

Terms that are very close to what you are looking, however they will not generate the type of high quality leads you are looking for.

- O Screens for replacement windows
- ✗ Window replacement warranty
- O Trailer home window replacement
- ✗ Commercial window replacement
- O Window cleaning company

You can see how certain terms completely change the purchase intent of the buyer. It's important to filter these related terms and ensure they don't trigger your ads.

Competition:

- O Home Depot replacement windows
- O Renewal by Anderson replacement windows

There's a good chance you can generate a lead or two by bidding on competitive traffic, however you'll discover it may be more of a hassle than it's worth. It is something to test, however, if you're set on trying it out. Refer back to my previous section about competitor traffic for more detailed information on this.

These are all examples of the different paths searchers take and how your ad may appear. It's always best practice to sit down and brainstorm all of the negative keywords that may trigger your ad and put them into a negative keyword list prior to launching a campaign. Save your money and focus your budget in the areas where you can generate leads.

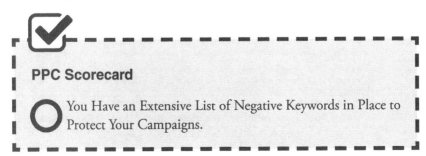

PPC Scorecard

O You Have an Extensive List of Negative Keywords in Place to Protect Your Campaigns.

PLAY #81 | **Control Your Bidding Strategy So You Don't Overpay for Leads**

Play Action:

Implement a Bidding Strategy To Get The Most Amount of Leads Without Spending More Than You Should.

You can control what you are willing to bid and pay for a given click.

Bidding is a fundamental component of pay-per-click.

As you may already know, pay-per-click on Google search is a live auction. Each search is a new auction with the opportunity for your ad to appear. You are essentially bidding against your competition and pay a different rate every time someone searches for your services and clicks on your ad.

Obviously, the higher you are willing to bid, the more exposure you will receive, the higher your ad positions will be and ultimately the faster you'll go through budget. The biggest mistake most advertisers make is not having control over their bidding. Google has many bidding options and strategies you can implement. They include fully automated bidding strategies and manual strategies.

 Steves PPC Breakdown

I always recommend starting out with a manual bidding strategy giving you 100% control over your bidding. This will provide you with greater visibility into what your competitive rates are in a given area. You can then adjust as needed once you have greater insight into a given market.

You can control your bids for each individual keyword.

Once you have conversion tracking setup and know how a given keyword performs, you can adjust your investment on an individual keyword basis. If a certain keyword becomes one of your top performers, you can invest more on it with confidence knowing it has a historically high performance.

You may have keywords in your portfolio that represent traffic very early in your sales funnel that produce traffic, but perform with a lower conversion. For these words you can bid less. On the other side of the coin, you may have a keyword that is performing really well for you but doesn't have any competition at all, which essentially allows you to name your own bid rate.

By having a combination of keywords at different rates and manually making bid adjustments at the keyword level you'll start to gain more efficiency in your account, your cost per lead will be more manageable, and you'll have a nice healthy portfolio of keywords at different rates generating at a greater return.

You can control your bids by time of day and by day of the week.

If you notice that certain days deliver more volume than others or certain times of day deliver more volume, you can increase your bids based on the historical performance of these factors. This works particularly well when you notice competition dropping off either later in the day or toward the end of the month when a competitor may run out of budget.

Dropping bids at these times will help you generate leads at a discount. You also want to pay close attention to a competitor's hours of operation. Do most of the competitors in your market shut ads down at a certain time? This gives you the opportunity to advertise in off hours and generate leads for the next business day.

You can control the device.

Another big mistake that advertisers make when it comes to bidding is not understanding which device pulls in the bulk of traffic and leads.

Do you spend 80% of your budget on desktop search but only generate 20% of your leads on that device?

Play #81 / Control Your Bidding Strategy So You Don't Overpay for Leads

Do the majority of your leads come in by way of a mobile device? You want to align your bidding strategy to the types of devices that pull in your best leads and opportunities. If 80% of your leads come in from mobile, than 80% of your budget should be applied there.

You can easily control the spend by device by making adjustments to bid modifiers in the device section in a given campaign. At the keyword level, Google gives you a complete break down of spending by device and how much a click and conversion cost by device as well.

fig. 81-1: Click and conversersion cost by device

Google gives you the flexibility and control to adjust your bid rates by a given location as well. If you advertise in more than one place and cover a number of zip codes you can control your bid rate by each location. Looking at historical sales information by either average transaction value or average revenue by a given location would be helpful in determining where you should invest more.

When it comes to location bidding it can be boiled down to three components:

- Bid higher in the areas with a proven track record in sales.

- Bid lower in mediocre or average areas.

- Drastically reduce bids or eliminate underperforming areas.

Business situations where you may need to adjust your bids:

    O When you get busy   O Seasonal sales

○ When you get slow   ○ Weekends

✗ When there is a weather   ✗ When you have a TV or
  event   radio campaign

○ Holidays

One of the easiest ways to manage bidding is by the keywords **overall average cost per click**. My personal rule of thumb is to make bidding adjustments to keywords for every 100 ad impressions for normal traffic generating keywords, every 1000 impressions for high volume keywords.

 Steve's PPC Breakdown

After evaluating the conversion performance (and once I am satisfied with a given position of a keyword) I will adjust the bid rate up or down based on the running average of the cost per click. If my bid rate is $20 for example and my average CPC is $18.95 over a 30-day running average with a consistent conversion, I will bid down to the $18.95 CPC and will continue this process as I achieve the lowest possible bid rate without impacting lead volume.

Bidding in Google Ads is not a blanketed strategy. Every keyword can be adjusted based on time and day performance, device performance, location performance, and you can move bids up and down based on different business situations.

Bidding is a constant testing ground and it's something that should be evaluated and adjusted weekly, if not daily. When in doubt follow the rule of averages and don't let traffic slip away.

PPC Scorecard

○ You Are Making Bidding Adjustments For Individual Keywords to Optimize Performance.

PLAY #82 | Control Ad Position and Improve Lead Quality

Play Action:

Test The Position of Your Ads. See Which Position Draws the Best Lead Quality.

In which position should your ads appear in order to get the greatest amount of leads? Is it first position, second position...fourth position? Should you have a greater position on mobile compared to desktop?

Google gives you all the information you need to make a decision on the position where your ad appears. You have the ability to control the position of your ads. The ad position is mostly controlled by your bidding rate, however it is possible to have a lower bid rate compared to a competitor and a higher position when you have a better overall quality score.

Every keyword in your portfolio has a certain 'sweet spot' where it performs the best. With ad position you want to take into consideration a few factors:

- O Lead volume
- O Lead cost
- O Lead quality
- O Messaging

You'll find in certain categories you'll have a great deal of lead volume in the first position, however you may compromise lead quality. There is a healthy balance of cost and position as it relates to lead quality.

Keep in mind your target audience when it comes to ad position, too. There's a good chance you want to do business with a smart prospect. Smart prospects like to weigh options and they carefully select the ads that they want to click on and pursue. That's why bidding is not the only thing that should be considered in your ad position. You also want to make sure you have really tight ad copy that attracts smart consumers.

If you show me an ad in the first position in any given market, I can show you an even better ad in the second or third position that yields not only a better cost, but also better overall qualified leads.

Messaging is huge. If you've taken the time and put in the effort following my Ad Copy Formula method, this is where you'll start to see that time investment begin to pay off. A better offer in a lower position will always outperform a higher ad position with a bad or irrelevant message.

You also want to consider the buying cycle of the prospect. If your prospect is looking for help today or you have a product and/or service with a low barrier to entry, the higher the position means the more leads you'll generate. It will be crucial to nab that top spot. If your product or service has a higher transaction value and takes more time to sell, a second to fourth position is where you want to be.

Think about it for a minute; if you're in the market for something substantial and search on Google, you are reading a few ads and scrolling down the page before you make a decision. Ad copy and positioning are elements you always want to test on a monthly basis so you can identify your sweet spot for a given service or product. Seek quality over quantity.

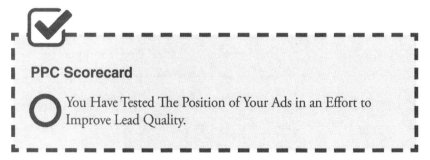

PPC Scorecard

◯ You Have Tested The Position of Your Ads in an Effort to Improve Lead Quality.

PLAY #83 | **Control Budget To Achieve a Healthy Cost Per Lead**

Play Action:

Properly Size Your Budget to Your Goals, Locations and Ad Schedule to Achieve a Balanced Lead Cost.

Most advertisers make the mistake of establishing a Google budget without really knowing or understanding how much search volume their market generates.

Google has come a long way with providing forecasts and historical information. You can now see right in the Google Keyword Planner exactly how much search volume a given keyword or portfolio of keywords delivered during a time frame in a given area. You can drill down to the zip code level. You're also able to see how competitive the keyword is with a range of low and high bid rates. This will give you the information you need to establish a budget that makes sense for your business.

With budget management there are a few rules to follow:

1. First, you want to make sure you have enough budget to sustain the entire time frame of a given campaign. If you run your campaign from 8am to 5pm you need to be able to support traffic during this time frame. This way you'll get the full benefit of fluctuations to bidding change throughout the course of the day.

2. Keep in mind, lead costs vary throughout the cycle of a given day, week, or even month. If you run out of budget early in the day you may have a higher cost per lead average than you

would if you had more budget. So having a bigger budget could actually help you keep your overall costs low.

3. Next, don't bite off more than you can chew. Size up your keyword portfolio and locations to your budget. If you have a $5,000/month budget and a keyword portfolio that can easily spend $10,000/month you should narrow your focus down to the keywords and locations that are in alignment with your budget. Trying to do too much with a limited budget can stunt your performance growth.

4. Always manage your budget manually. Google gives you two options when setting up your budget (monthly budget management and average daily budget) and this has changed over the past few years:

Monthly Budget Management

With a monthly budget, you set how much you want your campaign to spend over the course of a month. Your actual spend may vary each day, but by the end of the month you won't pay more than the monthly budget you set for the campaign. You'll see higher spend on days your ads are likely to see more traffic, balanced lower spend on other days but in a month you won't pay more than the monthly budget.

*When to pick this option- If your business conducts monthly financial planning, or otherwise needs guaranteed, accurate monthly spend, monthly campaign budgets are the better option. You'll be able to set how much you want your campaign to spend in a month.

Average Daily Budget

With an average daily budget, you set the average amount you would like to spend each day over the course of a month. While your actual spend may vary each day, in a month you won't pay more than your average daily budget multiplied by the average number of days in a month, which is 30.4.

On days when your ads are likely to be in higher demand, you may spend up to 2X your average daily budget. But those days are balanced by days when your spend is below your average daily budget, so over a month, you won't end up paying more than your average daily budget multiplied by 30.4

* When to pick this option- If your business prefers to focus on daily spend and wants to drive in more daily volume this may be a better option. For example, if you're advertising only on the weekends, and you want to only spend on those specific days, average daily budgets may work better for you.

Regardless of which budget strategy you choose you always want to manage and monitor your account daily and make adjustments based on the ebb and flow of your business.

PPC Scorecard

O You Have Implemented a Budget Strategy That is Properly Sized to Your Market So You Generate a Healthy Lead Cost. You Have Enough Budget to Cover Both the Locations You Want to Advertise In Along With The Ad Schedule.

PLAY #84 | Control Your Device Strategy to Get The Most Out of Your Budget

Play Action:

Understand Which Device Pulls In Your Best Leads and Put More Budget in The Areas That Deliver the Best Return.

If most of your budget is being spent on desktop search, but the majority of your high-quality leads and opportunities are being generated on mobile wouldn't it make sense to shift your budget to the areas that produce your best revenue? By doing this you'll make your budget work much harder for you.

First you need to know where your opportunities are coming from. Google provides you with all the information you need to clearly see which devices bring in your best leads. You just need conversion tracking properly setup.

In the devices section within your Google Ads account you can filter your view by device type. When you add the conversions column you can see how many leads you have generated on a mobile device. The majority of my local business clients generate about 70% of their leads on mobile.

	Device	Level	Added to	Bid adj.	Conversions
☐	Mobile phones	Campaign	RHEEM: PRODUCT FOCUS	+60%	47.00
☐	Mobile phones	Campaign	CARRIER: PRODUCT FOCUS	+60%	25.00
☐	Mobile phones	Campaign	GOODMAN: PRODUCT FOCUS	+60%	44.00
☐	Mobile phones	Campaign	PALM BEACH BMM KICKER: AC REPAIR COUNTY	+60%	68.00

fig. 84-1: Mobile bid modifier

You have the ability to control your advertising strategy based on the type of device you want to target. You want to align your budget and apply it to the devices that generate your best leads. For most local businesses with short sales cycles this is going to be on mobile.

The single biggest growing segment in search is mobile.

You can easily adjust and increase your bids for each of your ads based on the device type to achieve higher placement on mobile devices, desktop or tablets. If you want to maintain a desktop presence but want to spend more on mobile you can easily do this. Alternatively you can advertise on mobile exclusively. Google now gives you this flexibility with device bid adjustments. If you wanted to advertise exclusively on mobile you would set your desktop bid adjustment to -100%.

To see how your ads appear on different devices you can use the ad preview tool. Here you can see the display for mobile, desktop and tablets.

fig. 84-2: Google ad preview tool

Steves PPC Breakdown

The types of ads that work the best on mobile are going to be Expanded Text Ads with a call extension. This gives the searcher the option to click on your ad and go to your landing page or they can click on your call extension and bypass your landing page and call you. I've found this to be the most successful method in generating mobile leads.

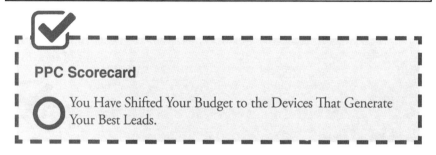

PPC Scorecard

You Have Shifted Your Budget to the Devices That Generate Your Best Leads.

"I've learned that something constructive comes from every defeat."

- Tom Landry

SECTION #9
$FIXING
PAY-PER-CLICK
PROBLEMS

PROACTIVELY TROUBLESHOOT PPC PROBLEMS AND TAKE ACTION IN ORDER TO CAPITALIZE ON YOUR INVESTMENT.

You'll Discover How To Tackle Your High Cost Per Lead, The Causes For Your Budget Running Out, Why You're Experiencing Low Lead Volume, How To Solve Low Click-Through Rate and Low Conversion Issues, And The Ways To Stop Out Of Area Traffic.

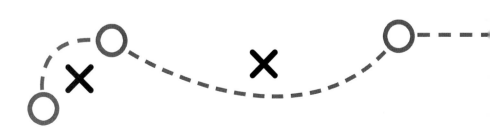

PLAY #85 | 10 Reasons Why Your Cost Per Lead is Too High and How To Fix It

Play Action:

Troubleshoot High Lead Costs and Follow These Optimization Strategies to Reduce Your Cost Per Acquisition.

○ Problem #1: Non Relevant Keywords Eating Away at Budget

Solution: Using the search terms report, look back at keywords that did not make sense and place them into a negative keyword list. Apply them to your campaigns so you will no longer be charged for them in the future.
See These Helpful Plays:
#4, #80

○ Problem #2: Ad Copy Does Not Match the Keyword

Solution: Rewrite your ad so it matches the buyer intent focusing all of the available space for that one keyword.
See These Helpful Plays:
#29, #47, #52, #81, #83

○ Problem #3: Ad Copy Became Stale

Solution: Much like the delicious fries you ate yesterday that just didn't taste the same today reheated, your ads go stale. Your ad that once produced a great result can all of a sudden stop being effective. That's why it's always a great idea to refresh your ad copy with new offers through ongoing split testing.
See These Helpful Plays:
#16, #29

Problem #4: Landing Page Copy is Not in Alignment with Ad Copy

Solution: Provide your prospect with a consistent experience by aligning your landing page copy with your ad.
See These Helpful Plays:
#50

Problem #5: Landing Page Technical Issues

Solution: Rule out any and all technical issues with your landing pages. This includes loading issues, issues you may have with display elements, or issues with speed. See how your landing page reacts on different browsers both on desktop and mobile.
See These Helpful Plays:
#52

Problem #6: Tracking System Issues

Solution: You may be generating leads and suffer a spike in a high cost per lead because one your tracking systems failed. Double check your call and form tracking ensure all your lines work correctly and everyone on your team is receiving form submissions.
See These Helpful Plays:
#5, #35

Problem #7: Not Enough Budget

Solution: You are exhausting your budget early in the day and not taking advantage of click costs where they are less competitive (later in the day when your competition gases out of budget). Increase your daily budget and adjust your timing or your locations in order to make your budget last longer. When you're able to apply more budget over an entire daily auction lifecycle your cost per lead will balance out.
See These Helpful Plays:
#77, #83

Problem #8: Ad Positioning

Solution: Your ad positioning may be too aggressive, so back down your bids in order to decrease your overall cost per click to drive in leads at a reasonable price.
See These Helpful Plays:
#82

Problem #9: Automated Bidding

Solution: Your bidding may be in a 'set and forget' automated setup with Google where they are maximizing your bid rate on every auction. As a result your lead costs are too high. Reset your bidding settings at the campaign level to manual bid management and establish a reasonable rate where you are in control of your bidding.
See These Helpful Plays:
#81

Problem #10: New Competition or Change to Competitor Strategy

Solution: A new competitor who comes into the playing field or one who changes their strategy and starts to compete against you by increasing bids can easily throw off your cost per lead. The best way to combat competitors is to have control of your bidding strategy. If both you and your competitor are setup on auto-bidding there's a good chance you are both raising prices and don't even realize it. It's done automatically through bid automation. It's always a good idea to control your outcome with manual bidding.
See These Helpful Plays:
#81

PPC Scorecard

You Have Troubleshooted High Lead Costs and Have Made Necessary Adjustments to Reduce Your Cost Per Lead.

PLAY # **5 Reasons Why You Are Running Out of Budget and How To Fix It**

Play Action:

Identify The Sources of Your Bleeding Budget and Make Adjustments to Get the Most Out of Your Ad Spend.

Problem #1: Your Non-relevant Keywords are Eating Away at Budget.

Solution: Use the search terms report to identify negative keywords.
See These Helpful Plays:
#4, #80

Problem #2: Your Bids are Too High.

Solution: Your ad positioning and bidding rate may be too aggressive, back down your bids and lower your ad position in order to decrease your overall cost per click and make your budget last longer throughout the day.
See These Helpful Plays:
#82

Problem #3: You're Stuck in an Automated Bidding Strategy

Solution: Remove your campaigns from fully automated bidding strategies. These can drive up click costs and leave you paying more.
See These Helpful Plays:
#81

Problem #4: Your Daily Budget is Set Too Low to Handle Lead Volume

Solution: Use the Google Keyword Planner to see if you're setting the right budget for your market. Adjust your daily budget if it's set too low to handle the amount of traffic in your market.
See These Helpful Plays:
#83

Problem #5: Your Budget is Spread Too Thin for the Market

Solution: Plug your keywords and campaigns into the Keyword Planning tool to see the real limit of your market. You can identify if you have too many locations or campaigns running for the budget you currently have.
See These Helpful Plays:
#11, #77

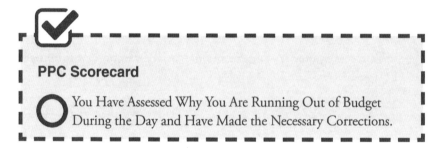

PPC Scorecard

You Have Assessed Why You Are Running Out of Budget During the Day and Have Made the Necessary Corrections.

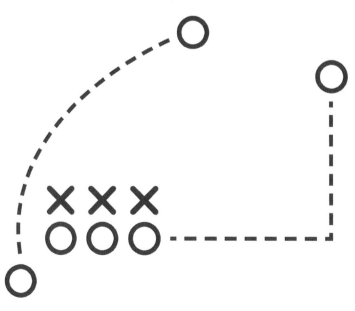

Play #86 / 5 Reasons Why You Are Running Out of Budget and How To Fix It

PLAY #87

7 Reasons Why You Are Experiencing Low Lead Volume and How To Fix It

Play Action:

Troubleshoot Common Causes of Decreased Traffic to Restore Your Lead Flow.

Problem #1: Conflicts in Your Keywords

Solution: Run a keyword diagnostic report to identify negative keywords blocking traffic. Remove them from your lists to ensure they aren't stopping your ads from showing.
See These Helpful Plays:
#2, #10

Problem #2: Conflicts in Your Geotargeting Strategy

Solution: You may be excluding an area from your location targets preventing traffic from a given area from seeing your ads. Using the ad preview tool, enter in the zip code along with the keyword delivering low leads to see if your ad appears.
See These Helpful Plays:
#77

Problem #3: Your Quality Score is Too Low.

Solution: Your keyword may have an underperforming quality score and as a result may not get the total impressions the market is delivering. Improve the keyword quality score by isolating the keyword to its' very own keyword ad group.
See These Helpful Plays:
#6, #7, #58

Problem #4: Low Bidding Rates or Low Positioning.

Solution: Raise your bids to ensure your ads are on the first page. Increase your quality score to earn a higher position. Try incrementally increasing your bid rate to increase your position and gain more leads.
See These Helpful Plays:
#3, #6, #81, #82

Problem #5: Bidding Conflicts in Your Strategy

Solution: Are you losing leads because your overall campaign strategy is out of sync? Identify places in your campaign where timing, location, or device settings may be holding back your best keywords.
See These Helpful Plays:
#76, #77, #84

Problem #6: Your Ads are Disapproved in Google Ads

Solution: Disapproval status can be caused by a variety of issues. Check your landing pages and that your keyword hasn't been disapproved by Google.
See These Helpful Plays:
#10, #58

Problem #7: A Low Traffic Day

Solution: Check on your best performing keywords and compare how they've historically done compared to today. If this is an outlier on your usual performance then just keep an eye out for a possible trend.
See These Helpful Plays:
#3

PPC Scorecard

You Have Assessed Why You Are Experiencing Low Lead Volume and Have Made the Necessary Corrections.

PLAY

5 Reasons Why You Have Low Click-Through Rate and No One is Clicking On Your Ads and How To Fix It

Play Action:

Get More Prospects to Click on Your Ad By Fixing Common Issues.

Problem #1: Your Campaign Traffic is Too Broad

Solution: Put negative keyword lists onto your campaigns to control traffic. Put your ads in front of customers who are likely to want your products or services.
See These Helpful Plays:
#4

Problem #2: Your Offers Are Not Compelling to Prospects

Solution: Test new versions of your ad with Google ad variations. If current offers aren't working, try reassessing them and follow the Ad Copy Formula to craft a killer offer every time.
See These Helpful Plays:
#16, #29

Problem #3: Your Once Top Performing Ad Has Gone Lame

Solution: If your ad no longer converts, you need to go back and adjust the ad copy. Test new versions of your ad with Google ad variations.
See These Helpful Plays:
#16, #29

Problem #4: Your Keyword is Not Relevant to the Ad Copy

Solution: A top performing ad will answer the needs of the searcher. If your keywords don't line up with the ads you've written or the intent of your prospects, go back and insert the keyword into your ad copy.

See These Helpful Plays:

#27

Problem #5: You Have Too Many Keywords in the Ad Group

Solution: Sift out top-performing keywords and put them into single keyword ad groups.

See These Helpful Plays:

#7

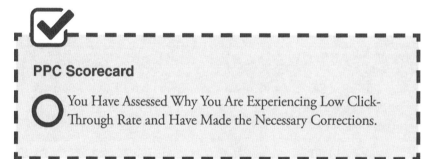

PPC Scorecard

You Have Assessed Why You Are Experiencing Low Click-Through Rate and Have Made the Necessary Corrections.

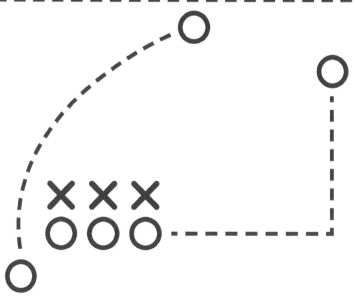

Play #88 / 5 Reasons Why You Have Low Click-Through Rate

PLAY

5 Reasons Why You Have Low Conversion and How To Fix It

Play Action:

Identify Reasons Why You are Getting Clicks But No Calls and Put a Plan Together to Increase Lead Conversion.

Problem #1: Your Landing Page has Technical Issues.

Solution: Check all technical aspects of the landing page. Speed issues, page loading elements issues, issues with browsers or device.
See These Helpful Plays:
#48, #52, #53,

Problem #2: Landing Page Message Does not Line up With Ads

Solution: When you design your landing page, make sure the message matches your ad exactly. Use the same offers as your ad copy and create a seamless experience for your customers.
See These Helpful Plays:
#50

Problem #3: You're Losing Prospects by Not Retargeting Them With Remarketing Campaigns

Solution: Deploy remarketing campaigns for longer sales cycle tickets or to cross-sell services to existing customers.
See These Helpful Plays:
#65, #66

Problem #4: Your Offers Are Not Compelling to Potential Customers

Solution: Assess if a weak offer is holding you back. Ensure your offer is solving the problems of your prospects and boldly promises them something to solve their needs.
See These Helpful Plays:
#16, #18, #21

Problem #5: Your Leads Are Being Improperly Handled.

Solution: Implement a call-tracking solution where you can record calls. Check them for quality and ensure your office is handling them the right way. Never advertise a promise you can't fulfill once a prospect calls.
See These Helpful Plays:
#24

PPC Scorecard

You Have Assessed Why You Are Experiencing Low Conversions and Have Made the Necessary Corrections.

PLAY **#90**

5 Reasons Why You are Not Getting Enough Traffic and How To Fix It

Play Action:

Identify Reasons Why You are Getting Traffic and Increase Search Impressions.

Problem #1: Your Keyword Strategy is Too Restrictive and Slows Traffic Volume

Solution: If you're running campaigns with only exact match keywords, this could be stunting your traffic flow. Add phrase match or broad match keywords to add more potential searches into your pool.
See These Helpful Plays:
#1, #11

Problem #2: You Aren't Advertising in Enough Locations

Solution: You may only be running your ads in a small area. Add more cities or zip codes into your campaigns. This will allow you to serve ads to more people and increase impressions.
See These Helpful Plays:
77

Problem #3: You've Set Your Targeting Settings Too Tight

Solution: Go into your campaign settings and see what demographic and audience targeting you have set up. You may be mistakenly excluding an audience or demographic you want to reach.
See These Helpful Plays:
#79

Problem #4: You Don't Have Enough Keywords in Your Account to Drive Sufficient Traffic

Solution: You may not be bidding on enough keywords. Go back to the drawing board. Use the Google Keyword Planner to search for opportunities to expand your keyword portfolio. Add new keywords to drive in more traffic and increase your impressions.

See These Helpful Plays:
#11

Problem #5: Your Bids are Too Low for Your Ads to Show Up on the First Page of Search Results

Solution: Pull up the keywords section of your account and filter by status. It will reveal what keywords are currently bidding too low to be on the first page and allow you to take corrective action.

See These Helpful Plays:
#10, #81

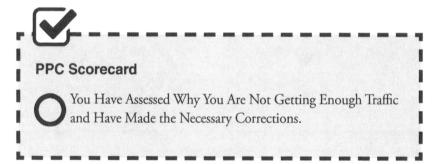

PPC Scorecard

You Have Assessed Why You Are Not Getting Enough Traffic and Have Made the Necessary Corrections.

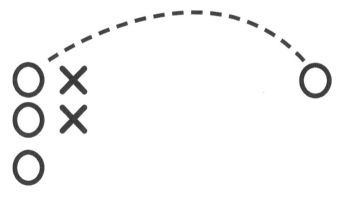

PLAY
#91
| Common Reasons Why You Are Generating Leads Outside Your Area and How To Fix It

Play Action:

Identify Why You are Generating Leads Outside Your Service Area and Tighten Up Your Geolocations.

Problem #1: You Did Not Set Up Geolocation Settings Correctly

Solution: You may be advertising in more places than you want. Go into your campaigns and click on the locations tab. You can see each town and zip code you're targeting here. If there's a location you don't want to be in, remove it from this list.
See These Helpful Plays:
#77

Problem #2: You're Not Excluding Specific Towns or Zip Codes from our Campaigns

Solution: If you keep receiving out of area calls, adding zip codes and towns to your exclusions will create an extra layer of protection. Go into your location settings and add unwanted locations to the exclusions list.
See These Helpful Plays:
#4, #77

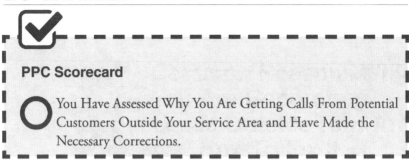

PPC Scorecard

You Have Assessed Why You Are Getting Calls From Potential Customers Outside Your Service Area and Have Made the Necessary Corrections.

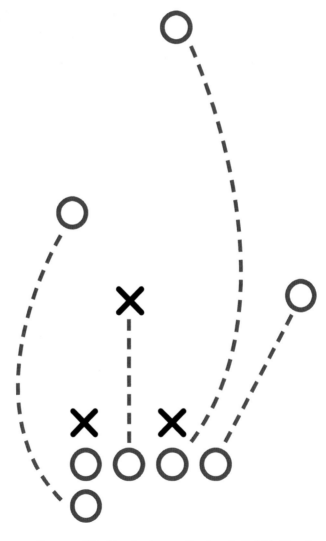

Play #91 / Common Reasons Why You Are Generating Leads Outside Your Area

"You're never a loser until you quit trying."

– Mike Ditka

"He who is not courageous enough to take risks will accomplish nothing in life."

- Muhammad Ali

SECTION #10
CHOOSING THE
RIGHT GOOGLE
PARTNER

EVALUATE YOUR CURRENT PPC MANAGER AND ENSURE THEY'RE TAKING STEPS TO IMPROVE YOUR LEAD GENERATION PROGRAM.

You'll Learn What Type Of Contract Structure To Be In, The Ideal Billing Relationship, How Transparent Your Current Provider Is, The Weekly And Monthly Account Management Checklists A Top PPC Manager Follows, And The Questions You Should Be Asking To Know You're With The Right Provider.

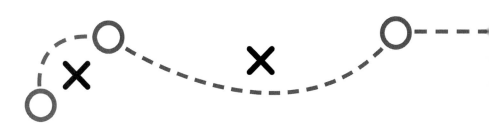

PLAY
#92

8 Questions To Ask A PPC Advertsing Agency Before You Hire Them

Play Action:

Assess Your Current PPC Management Contract and Know the Fine Print. What Is the Provider's Policies and are They Clear.

Contract Must Haves: Who Owns What?

- ○ No need to sign a long term contract.
- ○ Make sure fees are spelled out.
- ○ A direct bill relationship is always best- paying advertisers direct.
- ○ If you come to the table with an established account make sure you own it when you leave.

Contracts make sense when you purchase a home, acquire a business or secure financing. When it comes to advertising, you want to minimize your risk and protect your marketing budget. That's why it's important you never sign a long-term contract that locks you into an unproven relationship.

Most sales driven, pay-per-click companies are going to require a contract. This is how sales people make a commission, by locking you in. Any experienced PPC expert with a proven track record is not going to ask for a contract. They should be so confident in their ability to perform for you that a contract is not necessary.

A simple monthly agreement with deliverables and expectations in writing should be the extent of the document you agree to sign. At the same time, if you come to the table with a prebuilt Google Ads account with historical information you want to make sure you continue to own this account after a relationship is terminated.

Other Items to Consider in your PPC Management Contract:

1. Is there a minimum ad spend? The whole spirit of pay-per-click advertising is to pay for the clicks after you consume the benefit on a pay-as-you go model, paying Google direct. Be very cautious of companies who want you to pay all at once and upfront your ad entire spend.

2. Will the PPC Manager work with my competitors or will I have exclusively? If your budget can support all of the market volume, it would be in your best interest to work with a provider who will commit exclusively to your business so they don't have to make a choice on who will get the opportunities in a given area.

3. Are there any performance guarantees? You always want to protect your risk. Let's say you hand over a $5000 budget to a PPC Manager and you only get one lead. Obviously the execution was mishandled. What is your recourse in situations of malpractice?

4. Will I own the Google Ad Account? Unless the PPC provider comes to the table with a proprietary and proven PPC build for your industry you should own your account and all of the history.

5. Will I own my call tracking lines? Nowadays, it's easy to transfer lines to call tracking solutions and between carriers. You want to make sure if a phone line is being ordered and used in your PPC accounts that you own it if and when the agreement is terminated.

6. What is the service level? How often is the account being managed and what is included? My personal rule of thumb for any account I manage is to commit roughly 5-6 man hours of account management for every $5000 being invested. This includes a daily, weekly and monthly battle plan along with weekly check-in meetings with my clients.

7. Am I paying advertisers direct with access to confirm actual billing? You always want to pay your advertisers direct because you'll know that every dollar in ad spending will actually go to the advertiser and not to somebody else.

8. Will the PPC Manager make a hidden markup, commission or fee based on your ad spend? If you do decide to pay the advertiser direct (which I highly advise against) I would carefully read the agreement. Are you being charged a fixed fee or an approximate fee for PPC management services? This is important. You always want to know exactly what you are getting in a clear and transparent relationship.

Make sure to always read the fine print before committing to a PPC management agreement. Anybody can sell you PPC management services. The agreement will help you ensure you are not lied to, cheated or neglected and if you are, you will have immediate recourse to leave.

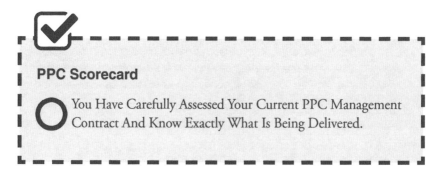

PPC Scorecard

O You Have Carefully Assessed Your Current PPC Management Contract And Know Exactly What Is Being Delivered.

PLAY #93

What is Your PPC Billing Arrangement? What Level of Access and Transparency Do You Receive?

Play Action:

You Have Direct Access to Your Accounts, an Accurate Dashboard, and You Pay Advertisers Directly.

Google Account Access, Dashboard and Reporting:

O Trust but verify any data you receive.

X Reconcile your Google charges in the invoicing section directly inside Google Ads. Your credit card statement should match up to what you are being charged here.

X When you pay your Manager direct instead of the advertiser direct you lose this level of transparency.

O Beware of agencies that have hidden markups, or make commissions or percentages of spend without your knowledge.

O Understand your fees and your access level.

There are plenty of cool looking reporting and dashboard software solutions out there that can display your PPC performance. This technology can be used for good and it can also be *used for evil*. Almost all of these solutions have a built-in tool that takes the true click cost and **marks it up**, the click costs you see may not actually be the actual amount. Unfortunately, this is how some agencies make a secondary source of profit- from your ad spend, often without your knowledge.

To eliminate any concerns or improprieties you should be given access to your advertising accounts so you can monitor performance, verify that your service level agreement is being properly delivered, and oversee your budget.

Your credit card statement should match up to the invoicing you find inside the advertising account. When you have access to the advertising account there will never be any question about how funds are being applied to your growth. With this kind of system of checks and balances you'll never be in a situation where you'll be taken advantage of.

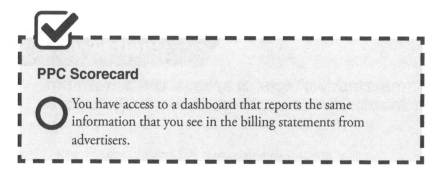

PPC Scorecard

You have access to a dashboard that reports the same information that you see in the billing statements from advertisers.

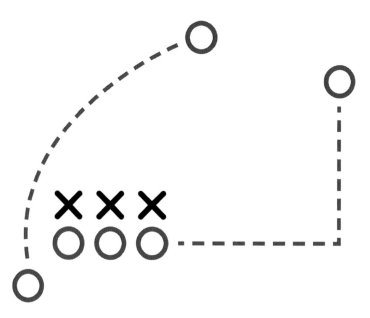

Play #93 / What is Your PPC Billing Arrangement?

PLAY #94 | **[Checklist] Is the PPC Account Being Managed With The Latest and Most Up-To-Date Technology?**

Play Action:

Your PPC Manager Uses Modern Advertising Technology to Keep You Competitive. They Send Your Traffic to Optimized, Responsive Landing Pages to Increase Lead Volume.

Google Advertising Technologies

1. **Remarketing**: The ability to retarget users who have visited your website or landing pages across the Google Display network with graphic ads.

2. **Remarketing Lists For Search Ads**: Similar to traditional remarketing, only these ads show up in the Google search results. It tracks a customer coming back into the sales funnel.

3. **Keyword Level Conversion Tracking**: You're able to track how each keyword performs by installing a script onto your landing pages and setting this up through the Google Ads account.

4. **Google Analytics & Google Tag Manager Integration**: Actively tracking user information and activity on your website and landing pages. Uses tag manager to allow for new conversion tags to be set quickly.

5. **Responsive Search Ads**: Ads that use machine learning to test thousands of ad variations using just 15 headlines and 4 descriptions. Google then automatically serves the best performing ads.

6. **Customer Match Advertising**: Use a list of current customers uploaded directly to Google so you can target them.

7. **Pay For Performance Display Advertising**: Using Google's Display Network to display ads on over 2 million websites. This campaign can be set so you only pay for acquisitions- not for clicks.

8. **In-Market Audience Targeting**: Predicts a consumer's intent and allow you to target hot prospects who are interested in your services or products.

9. **Pay Per View YouTube Advertising**: You are charged per 1,000 views of the ad, which can help you control costs for video advertising.

10. **Click Fraud Blocking**: The ability to identify and get refunds for invalid clicks in your ads account.

Landing Page Element

A good PPC strategy includes the use of landing pages. A landing page helps you drastically improve your lead conversion when compared to sending your prospect to a home page after they click on an ad. A landing page will also **NOT** interfere with any SEO you may already be investing in. There are a number of questions to consider when evaluating your landing pages:

○   How fast will my landing pages load?

✗   Where is it hosted?

✗   What happens if the server fails? Will my ads continue to run?

○   Will you customize the landing pages so it looks and feels like my business or do you use boilerplate templates?

○   Are you building an individual landing pages for each of my cities and campaigns to help improve lead conversion and Google Quality Score?

○   Are you using local phone numbers on my pages?

✗   How does your landing page technology manage leads?

✗   Can I add in videos, reviews, coupons or other custom elements?

○   Will it work with mobile search?

○   How does your form technology work?

○   Are you setting up remarketing on my landing pages?

Responsive Landing Page Technology

1. Landing pages are branded to your company, designed to build trust with potential customers, are designed to look clean, bright, friendly, and interactive, along with working on all devices.

2. Server, security and speed: Your landing pages are fast, are built with a secure SSL certificate, are routinely backed-up and run on dedicated managed servers.

3. Click intelligence: Your are using click tracking software to identify visitors on your site, to reveal the IP address, position of ad, keyword, device, and location of visitor.

4. Call tracking, specifically dynamic keyword call tracking, is being used to track keyword performance.

5. Forms are properly styled for both desktop and the customer mobile experience. They easily collect information and you are using form-to-call technology that automatically calls you and the prospect at the same time so you can instantly connect while they are still hot on page.

6. You are receiving instant lead notifications either by text message or email to track, monitor, and manage leads coming into your organization. You are also receiving alerts when a lead does not connect.

7. Your PPC Manager is using a CRO solution like heat mapping technology. It's similar to an instant replay system, where it records the session of a user to identify problem areas and opportunities for improvement.

PPC Scorecard

◯ Your Provider Is Using the Latest Advertising Technology in Your Campaigns and Landing Pages to Improve Your Performance.

PLAY
#95

What Are You Paying For? Is Your PPC Account in a Set and Forget Relationship or is Your Account Actually Being Managed?

Play Action:

You Can Verify That Your PPC Manager is Actively Managing Your Account Performance- Not Being Left on Autopilot.

Your Daily PPC Management Checklist- The PPC Accounting Method

1. **Your account is receiving daily keyword maintenance including:**

    ○ Negative keyword additions.

    ✕ Optimize top performing keywords into SKAGS.

    ○ Optimize under performers.

    ○ Remove non-performing keywords.

2. **Keywords Are Receiving Bid Adjustments**

    ○ Bids are increased for position to increase lead volume.

    ○ Bid rates are optimized for better efficiency.

    ✕ Bid rates are optimized for better search impression share.

    ○ Bids are being managed by device, time and location.

3. **Budgets Are Being Managed Daily**

    ○ Adjust budgets based on market volume and your lead generation goals.

4. **Competition is Analyzed**

   O   Competition search impression share reporting indicates how much search volume you are receiving compared to your competitors.

   X   Competition offers are examined for changes or updates.

   O   Identify competitors who have changed positioning or have fallen off in an effort to understand their spending habits.

5. **Identify New Opportunities**

   X   Implement new keyword opportunities.

6. **Improve Low Volume Keywords**

   X   Adjust bids for low volume keywords where you have potential business but are not in a position to compete for it with low click volume.

7. **Make Any Necessary Repairs**

   O   Administrative updates to credit card details.

   X   Landing pages requiring approvals.

   O   Any campaigns that did not achieve a desired result.

   X   Work on campaigns with a higher than normal cost per lead.

Here are Some Additional Questions You Can Ask Your PPC Manager

How Do You Manage My Bids? Are You Using Google's Automatic Bidding Or Are You Managing Them Manually?

Automatic bidding is a strong sign that your PPC company is placing you on a set-and-forget path. Typically automatic bidding will inflate your costs and gives Google a blank check to bleed your budget dry. Manual bid management is the best choice because it means a set of eyes is looking at individual keyword performance and making changes at the keyword level, helping you make your budget as efficient as possible.

How Often Are You Reviewing Click Activity And What Actions Are You Taking To Improve My Keyword Performance?

The very foundation of pay-per-click advertising starts with keywords. You are paying for the clicks made by prospects who take action on your ads. These ads are triggered by the search terms they type into the search engine. These are your keywords. That is why it is important for keyword performance management to be completed every day. It's a simple task that can save you thousands over the course of a year. Good keywords should be isolated and new campaigns should be designed for your top performing keywords. Keywords that are not performing should be tested with different ads or in different positions. Keywords that don't make sense to your sales funnel should be immediately moved to a negative keyword list to prevent any future waste.

It's this daily process of refinement and optimization that helps fine tune your lead quality and improves your acquisition costs. Google has a number of reports that will show you exactly how a PPC expert works your account. The Search Terms Report shows you all of the clicks you have paid for along with actions taken on each keyword. And the **Change History Report** shows you all of the time stamped actions taken on your account.

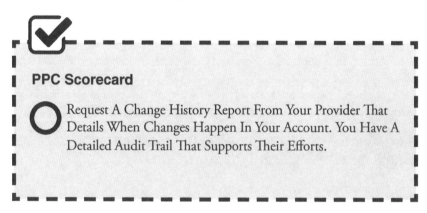

PPC Scorecard

O Request A Change History Report From Your Provider That Details When Changes Happen In Your Account. You Have A Detailed Audit Trail That Supports Their Efforts.

PLAY #96 | **Weekly PPC Management Checklist- Ad Copy Maintenance**

Play Action:

Your Provider Consistently Tests Your Ad Copy and Uses New Formats to Ensure Your Ads Stay Relevant and Maintain High Performance Standards.

How Often Are You Split Testing My Ads?

You should never have the same ad running with your PPC Manager as when you first started. In fact, you should start out your campaigns with 2-3 competing ads. Google will report back as to which one delivers a better result. Just like top performing race horses lose their edge, an ad goes lame overtime if it doesn't get updated. You may have an ad that really works one day and doesn't deliver any results for you the next. That's why it's important to split test ads for keywords at every 100 search impressions. When you do this you'll start to see a constant improvement with your click-through-rates which means you're getting the most traffic you can from the available search volume.

Are Low Quality Score Ads Being Improved?

At the keyword level there is a quality score column where Google grades your ad relevance. On a weekly level you want to sort through any and all relevances that are below average and make immediate improvements in an effort to improve quality score.

Are You Setup Using Google's Responsive Ads?

Responsive Search Ads help you automate ad performance, helping you increase click-through rates by automatically testing your messaging in your market. Using this ad format will help you identify which messaging is the most appealing for your business.

Are You Setup Using Google's Ad Extensions?

Ad extensions deliver a whole new level of performance to your advertising. They help you strengthen your message and pave the way to higher click-through rates and improved lead quality. On a weekly basis they should be tested, edited, and implemented in an effort to improve CTR.

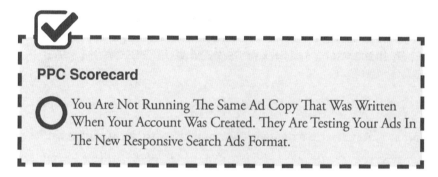

PPC Scorecard

You Are Not Running The Same Ad Copy That Was Written When Your Account Was Created. They Are Testing Your Ads In The New Responsive Search Ads Format.

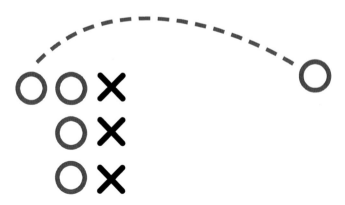

Play #96 / Weekly PPC Management Checklist- Ad Copy Maintenance

PLAY
#97

Monthly PPC Management Checklist

Play Action:

The Provider Performs Monthly Account Maintenance Tasks That Lead to Improvements. You Are Being Provided Metrics on a Monthly Basis to Assess Success and Make an Account Plan.

1. **Audience Management**

   Add/edit/update Google Ads audiences- you can apply more budget to the audiences that are performing the best.

2. **Location Management**

   After reviewing financial data- look at average transaction value by zip code or a list of top performing zip codes. See where you can apply budget in the areas that deliver your best revenue while reducing lower performing areas.

3. **Conversion Rate Optimization**

   Using instant replay or heat map technology to identify opportunities for landing page improvements including changes to page elements or correcting technical issues.

4. **Prepare Google Click Quality Review**

Submit refund requests for out of area or clicks resulting from fraud

5. **Verify Google Optimization Scores are 100%**- Google grades each of your campaigns using artificial intelligence. Your PPC Manager can accept or reject Google's recommendations to make improvements to your account. A 100% optimization score verifies this is being done properly.

6. Prepare Metrics for Client:
   - O Cost per lead
   - ✗ Conversion rate
   - O Click-through rate
   - O Positioning
   - ✗ Competition
   - O Search impression share
   - O Invalid click activity

How Often Are You Optimizing My Landing Pages?

The person you hire should have access to a landing page heat map tool they use to help you improve your lead conversion. Software like this collects data on where your prospects engage with your landing pages the most, where they fall off, what prevents them from taking action and how long they stay on the page. A good heat map solution will also record the visitor interaction in the form of a video that can be reviewed. With this information, your PPC Manager can determine which conversion elements are driving in revenue and what components of your landing pages need to be adjusted to improve lead conversion.

Keep in mind, once a prospect clicks on your ads, you've already paid for the click. The job of the landing page is to take that click and turn it into a lead. The higher it converts, the more leads you will get at a lower cost. It is quite possible to generate more leads without having to spend more on advertising when you actively optimize your landing pages. In the trade, this is called conversion rate optimization or CRO.

PPC Scorecard

You Have A Monthly Management Call Which Discusses Key Performance Metrics And A Plan To Address Underperforming Campaigns.

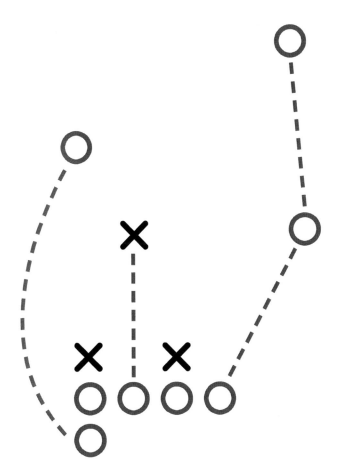

Play #97 / Monthly PPC Management Checklist

PLAY
#98

Is Your PPC Manager Tracking Individual Keyword Level Conversion Performance?

Play Action:

Verify That Your PPC Manager Uses Keyword Level Tracking to Record how Each Keyword Performs.

Are You Set Up Using Conversion Tracking Within Google Adwords And Tracking Individual Keyword Performance?

Setting up conversion tracking is an advanced strategy to track the lead conversion on individual keywords. Without conversion tracking installed, your PPC Manager is relying completely on instincts and unproven data to see how a keyword is performing.

To setup conversion tracking you need to have a call tracking solution with keyword-level tracking functionality, you need Google Analytics, and you need to integrate these two technologies into both your landing pages and Google Ad account to close the loop and track your individual keyword performance.

Once you do this and know what works and what doesn't work, your PPC Manager can take action to improve your performance and optimize your return on ad spend. Every single keyword has its own ROI. Over time, historical conversion tracking will paint a picture of your best times and days. Your PPC Manager will be able to use this data to craft a customized strategy to eliminate waste and improve your lead generation performance.

PPC Scorecard

O Your PPC Manager Uses Individual Keyword Conversion To Track Your Success. They Have Implemented All Necessary Technical Aspects To Ensure Accuracy.

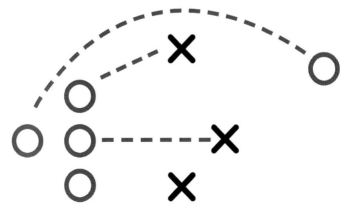

Play #98 / Is Your PPC Manager Tracking Individual Keyword Performance?

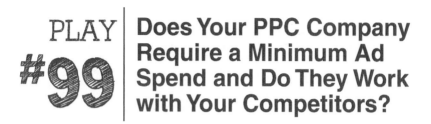

PLAY

#99

Does Your PPC Company Require a Minimum Ad Spend and Do They Work with Your Competitors?

Play Action:

Ensure Your PPC Manager Has You Set Up With A Direct Billing Arrangement And Works Only With You.

Do You Require a Minimum Advertising Commitment and How Do You Pay For The Advertising?

The beautiful thing about pay-per-click is that you only pay when somebody clicks on your ads- after it happens. That's why it is important for you to know that anyone asking for a monthly minimum committed spend is most likely making a hidden markup or commission on your advertising budget. One of the telltale signs is if you are writing them a check directly for advertising and not to the advertising source like Google, Bing, or Facebook.

When you advertise on Google, you should be invoiced and billed direct by Google **NOT** by the person or company managing your campaigns. An ethical PPC expert is going to charge you either a flat rate or a fixed percentage of spend to manage your account. They will set you up with a direct billing relationship with all advertisers. With this type of relationship, you are cutting out the middleman and you are protecting your ad spend. As a result, your budget will reach its fullest potential. You'll have 100% transparency and control in this type of arrangement.

At the same time you want to make sure your PPC Manager works for you and you alone. Having access to a competitor's account can really hurt your performance, especially when the budgets are similar in size. They ultimately have to pick a horse to win that day.

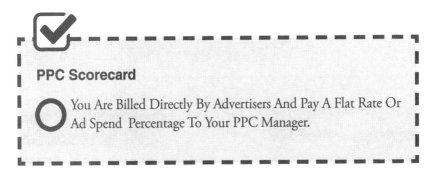

PPC Scorecard

O You Are Billed Directly By Advertisers And Pay A Flat Rate Or Ad Spend Percentage To Your PPC Manager.

Play #99 / Does Your PPC Company Require a Minimum Ad Spend?

PLAY #100

Is Your PPC Manager on Vacation? How Long Does it Take to Get Something Done?

Play Action:

Get into a Proactive, Not Reactive Meeting Schedule with Your PPC Manager.

How Often Will You Be Meeting With Me To Achieve Our Goals?

A great PPC expert will meet with you on a bi-monthly or monthly basis to discuss new opportunities, competitive situations, review your budget and ad performance, and share with you strategies that will impact your revenue. Cruise control with no changes should not be the expectation.

I like to meet with my clients once a week in a quick check-in meeting. My company also has a live help desk where clients can submit tickets for same day response, adjustments and changes.

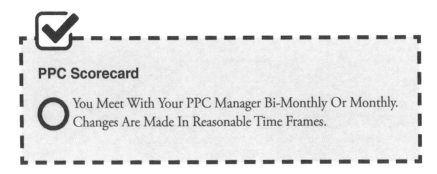

PPC Scorecard

O   You Meet With Your PPC Manager Bi-Monthly Or Monthly. Changes Are Made In Reasonable Time Frames.

PLAY #101

Does Your PPC Manager Really Get Your Business and Know Your Industry?

Play Action:

You're Working with a PPC Manager who has Experience and a Proven Track Record. They're Investing in Technology and Systems Which Support Your Business.

Qualifications You Need to Look For:

- O Years of experience doing lead generation.
- O Status with Google.
- O Industry experience.
- O Training programs for employees.

How much experience does your PPC Manager have? Anybody can go out and get a Google Ad Certification. It's a lot like getting a driver's license. All you have to do is take a test and for the most part all of the answers are available online. Yet, if you have ever taken a ride on your local highway I'm sure you'll agree that some people are just **not** cut out to drive. The same holds true to managing your PPC account. You want to make sure the person you hire has a proven track record of success.

Here are some things you should look for:

First, ask them how much advertising budget they manage as a company on an annual basis along with how many leads they generate. Take this number and divide it into the spend. This will tell you what their average cost per lead is client wide.

Next, ask for a copy of their company's monthly call tracking invoice. Any good PPC expert is going to have a call tracking company they work with to track your success. On the invoice you should look for how many phone lines they manage on behalf of their clients along with the number of minutes they are being charged for. When you see a lot of volume, this is a very good sign that this PPC expert is driving in leads for their clients.

Next, look for webinars, blogs, informative articles about PPC strategies, news and tips they author. Go to Amazon and search their name to see if they have any published documents like reports or even a book. This will tell you if they are really passionate about their craft and are staying on top of things.

Next you want to see how the PPC expert is affiliated with Google. When you are the best in your class, Google rewards you with Premier Partner Status. This status is a credential that proves the PPC expert is managing client accounts to best practices and has strong overall retention. Only a select number of companies achieve this status with Google.

And finally, ask them what percentage of your monthly management fee is actually applied to supporting software systems and technology. You want to see how much they invest in the latest software. Good software isn't cheap and if they don't have the cutting edge tools they are most likely not going to be able to compete on your behalf at the same level with others who do have access to these tools.

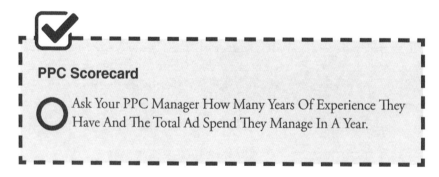

PPC Scorecard

Ask Your PPC Manager How Many Years Of Experience They Have And The Total Ad Spend They Manage In A Year.

GAME OVER

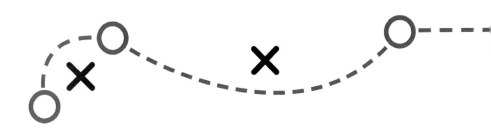

Download The PPC Scorecard and Receive Exclusive Access to Additional Resources

Just to say thanks for reading my book, I would like to give you the PPC Scorecard that goes along with each chapter **PLUS** exclusive access to tools, resources and training.

Go To: registerppcbook.com to access the materials.

THE PPC BOOK SCORE CARD

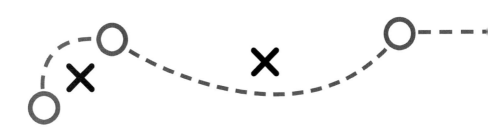

SECTION 1

O **PLAY #1**
Non-Relevant Keywords Draining Ad Budget on the Keyword Search Terms Report Have Been Identified and Blocked to Prevent Future Wasted Ad Spend.

O **PLAY #2**
Broad Match Modified Keywords are Being Used to Control Lead Quality and Wasted Ad Budget.

O **PLAY #3**
The Daily PPC Accounting System Has Been Implemented to Improve Keyword Performance: Focusing Budget on Top Performing Keywords, Troubleshooting Underperforming Keywords and Assigning Keywords Draining Ad Budget to Negative Keyword Lists.

O **PLAY #4**
Negative Keyword Lists Have Been Implemented To Prevent Bad Quality Traffic and Increased Click Costs.

O **PLAY #5**
Keyword Level Conversion Tracking Has Been Implemented to Track Individual Keyword Lead Generation Performance.

O **PLAY #6**
Low Quality Score Keywords Have Been Identified and Action is Being Taken to Optimize Ads and Improve Landing Pages in an Effort to Increase Quality Score Performance

O **PLAY #7**
Single Keyword Ad Groups Have Been Created For Focused Management and Continuous Improvement.

O **PLAY #8**
You Have Reviewed The 5 Keyword Reports to Identify Opportunities for Market Share Improvement. 1) Impression Share 2) Search Lost Top Impression Share Due to Rank 3) Search Top Impression Share 4) Search Absolute Top Impression Share 5) Click Share.

O **PLAY #9**
You Have Set Up Your Campaigns at the Local City Level so You Can Track Competitor Movement by Zip Code Using Google's Auction Insights Report.

O **PLAY #10**
You Have Identified All Keywords Not Eligible to Run By Running a Keyword Diagnostic Report and Have a Plan to Fix Them.

O **PLAY #11**
You Have Identified Your Market Potential and Have Correctly Sized up Your Budget to Capture Additional Sales Opportunities Using Google's Keyword Planning Tool.

O **PLAY #12**
You Have Implemented Location-Based Search Campaigns Focused on Mobile Devices to Attract Buyers Wanting to do Business with a Local Professional.

O **PLAY #13**
You Have Implemented a Voice Search Campaign to Capture the Growing Audience of Potential Customers Who Use Voice Assistants.

O **PLAY #14**
You Have Implemented Keyword Insertion For The Keywords Where you Do Not Have a Unique Ad.

O **PLAY #15**
You Have Reviewed Google's Campaign Recommendations and Have Accepted or Dismissed Their Recommendations.

SECTION 2

O **PLAY #16**

Adjust Your Ads So They Do Not Restrict Your Sales Goals. Create Compelling Messages that Include Benefits, Are Unique in Your Market, Include an Irresistible Offer and Make it Easy for Buyers to Take the Next Step in Your Sales Process.

O **PLAY #17**

Your Ad Copy Contains a Clear Call-To-Action

O **PLAY #18**

Your Ad Copy Contains a Speed Component.

O **PLAY #19**

Your Ad Copy Contains a Value Component Where You are Setting Yourself Apart From Your Competition.

O **PLAY #20**

Your Ad Copy Contains the Primary Benefits Associated With Your Products or Services.

O **PLAY #21**

Your Ad Copy Contains Risk Reversal and Clearly States a Bold Promise or Guarantee.

O **PLAY #22**

Your Ad Copy Contains The Number of Positive Reviews, Includes a Trusted 3rd Party and/or Mentions The Total Number of Years in Business.

O **PLAY #23**

Your Ad Copy Contains The City Names and Local Phone Lines For The Areas you Are Targeting.

O **PLAY #24**

You Have Removed Barriers in Your Sales Process, Making it Easy For Buyers to do Business With You.

○ **PLAY #25**

You Are Positioning All of the Unique Ways You Are Different in Your Sales Copy.

○ **PLAY #26**

You Have a Deadline on Your Offers to Accelerate Sales.

SECTION 3

○ **PLAY #27**

You Have Supporting Ads and Landing Pages Built Out For Each of Your Individual Product and Service Offering Categories.

○ **PLAY #28**

You Have Identified All Low Click-Through Rates and Have Put a Plan in Place to Improve CTR Performance.

○ **PLAY #29**

You Have Implemented Google's Ad Variation Tool to Test and Improve Your Ad Copy Messaging in an Effort to Increase Click-Through Rate.

○ **PLAY #30**

All of Your Ads Are Setup on Expanded Text Ads With 3 Headlines and 2 Description Lines.

○ **PLAY #21**

Implement Google's New Responsive Search Ads to Improve Click-Through Rate and Reduce CPC.

○ **PLAY #22**

Setup and Test Google's Gallery Ad Format For Services or Products That Have a Visually Appealing Outcome.

○ **PLAY #33**

Evaluate Your Mobile Advertising Strategy and Identify Any Active Call Only Ads. Split Test These Campaigns Against Expanded Text Ads to See Which Ad Format Has the Best Performance.

○ **PLAY #34**

You Have Shut Off Google Ad Extension Automation to Prevent Poor Ad Quality.

○ **PLAY #35**

You Have Shut Off Automated Google Call Reporting to Prevent Loss of Future Call Opportunities and to Provide Buyers With a Local Line They Trust.

○ **PLAY #36**

You Are Actively Monitoring Competitive Movement in Your Market.

SECTION 4

○ **PLAY #37**

Your Ads Are Setup Using Callout Extensions.

○ **PLAY #38**

Your Ads Are Setup Using Phone Call Extensions.

○ **PLAY #39**

Your Ads Are Setup Using Sitelink Extensions.

○ **PLAY #40**

Your Ads Are Setup Using Structured Snippets.

○ **PLAY #41**

You've Tested Message Extensions on Your Mobile Ads.

○ **PLAY #42**

You've Implemented Location Extensions to Drive Traffic to your Retail Location.

O **PLAY #43**
You've Implemented Price Extensions on Your Branded Campaigns.

O **PLAY #44**
You've Implemented Promotion Extensions to Highlight a Special Offer.

O **PLAY #45**
You're Actively Collecting Customer Reviews to Enhance Your Seller / Review Ratings.

O **PLAY #46**
You've Watched The Structure of a Top Performing Google Ad Video At REGISTERPPCBOOK.COM.

SECTION 5

O **PLAY #47**
Your PPC Strategy Includes the Use of Dedicated Landing Pages and You Have a Target Conversion Metric to Manage to.

O **PLAY #48**
Your Landing Pages Are Fast, Have a Clean Look and Feel, Are Using Friendly Colors, Are Using Only a Handful of Conversion Elements, Have No Navigation Elements and Are Setup to Prevent Technical Issues.

O **PLAY #49**
Your Landing Pages Are Responsive and the Mobile Experience Includes Easy to Use Features Like Click-to-Call and Mobile Stylized Forms.

O **PLAY #50**
Your Landing Page Messaging is Consistent with Your Ad Copy Messaging.

○ **PLAY #51**

Your Landing Pages Include the Right Mix of Text, Video and Imagery to Appeal to Different Buyer Types.

SECTION 6

○ **PLAY #52**

Your Landing Pages Run on a Dedicated Server, Have a Disaster Recovery Plan and are Protected From Threats.

○ **PLAY #53**

You Pulled a Google Speed Score Directly From Your Google Ads Account in the Landing Page Section. You are Implementing Speed Optimization Improvements to Enhance Your Prospect Experience to Drive in More Leads.

○ **PLAY #54**

You Have Implemented ValueTrack Parameters In Order To Track the Unique Details of Every Click.

○ **PLAY #55**

Your PPC Landing Pages Are Setup With Dynamic Keyword-Level Call Tracking.

○ **PLAY #56**

You Are Using Dynamic Landing Page Technology to Manage The Unique Messaging Your Website Visitors See on Your Landing Pages.

○ **PLAY #57**

You Are Using Heat Mapping Technology to Study How Visitors Interact with Your Landing Pages so You Can Make Conversion Rate Optimization (CRO) Improvements.

○ **PLAY #58**

You Have Identified All Below Average Landing Page Scores and Have Taken Action to Improve Overall Quality Score.

O **PLAY #59**
Implement Keyword Level Conversion Tracking To Get Individual Keyword Lead Cost Performance.

O **PLAY #60**
You Are Identifying Click Fraud and Requesting Click Credits From Google By Tracking IP Addresses on Your Landing Page.

O **PLAY #61**
Google Analytics and Google Tag Manager are Both Setup and Installed on Your Landing Pages.

O **PLAY #62**
Lead Conversion is Actively Being Measured.

SECTION 7

O **PLAY #63**
You've Setup a Google Search Advertising Account.

O **PLAY #64**
You've Setup a Google Display Campaign and You are Generating Leads on a Pay-Per-Lead Basis.

O **PLAY #65**
You Have an Active Remarketing Campaign Running on the Google Display Network.

O **PLAY #66**
You Are Running RLSA Ads to Recapture Opportunities and to Lower Lead Costs.

O **PLAY #67**
You Are Running YouTube Remarketing TrueView Pay-Per-View Ads.

O **PLAY #68**
You Are Running a Branded PPC Campaign.

○ **PLAY #69**
You Are Running a Google Customer Match Campaign to Generate Repeat Sales From Your Existing Customers.

○ **PLAY #70**
You Are Using Google's In-Market Audiences to Target Buyers in Your Market.

○ **PLAY #71**
You Are Running a Microsoft Ads Campaign on Bing, Yahoo and AOL to generate lower cost leads, complimenting your Google PPC strategy.

○ **PLAY #72**
You Have Installed a Facebook Pixel on Your Landing Pages and Website.

○ **PLAY #73**
You Have Installed the LinkedIn Tracking Script on Your Landing Pages and Website.

○ **PLAY #74**
You Have Created an LSA Account And Have Started The Process of Getting Google Guaranteed.

○ **PLAY #75**
You Have Turned Off The Google Search Partners Network in Your Campaign Settings to Avoid Budget Bleeding.

SECTION 8

○ **PLAY #76**
You Have Adjusted the Timing of your Campaigns to Run on The Days and Time Where You Get The Best Performance.

○ **PLAY #77**
You Have Built Out Campaigns at a Local Level in Order to Control Lead Cost, Target Your Best Performing Areas, and Appear as the Local Go-To Choice.

O **PLAY #78**
You Have Implemented a Competitor's Negative Keyword List to Prevent Bad Quality Traffic From Clicking on Your Ads.

O **PLAY #79**
Your Google Campaigns Include Google's Targeting Controls Where you Target or Restrict a Given Audience.

O **PLAY #80**
You Have an Extensive List of Negative Keywords in Place to Protect Your Campaigns.

O **PLAY #81**
You Are Making Bidding Adjustments For Individual Keywords to Optimize Performance.

O **PLAY #82**
You Have Tested The Position of Your Ads in an Effort to Improve Lead Quality.

O **PLAY #83**
You Have Implemented a Budget Strategy That is Properly Sized to Your Market So You Generate a Healthy Lead Cost. You Have Enough Budget to Cover Both the Locations You Want to Advertise In Along With The Ad Schedule.

O **PLAY #84**
You Have Shifted Your Budget to the Devices That Generate Your Best Leads.

SECTION 9

O **PLAY #85**
You Have Troubleshooted High Lead Costs and Have Made Necessary Adjustments to Reduce Your Cost Per Lead.

O **PLAY #86**
You Have Assessed Why You Are Running Out of Budget During the Day and Have Made the Necessary Corrections.

O PLAY #87

You Have Assessed Why You Are Experiencing Low Lead Volume and Have Made the Necessary Corrections.

O PLAY #88

You Have Assessed Why You Are Experiencing Low Click-Through Rate and Have Made the Necessary Corrections.

O PLAY #89

You Have Assessed Why You Are Experiencing Low Conversions and Have Made the Necessary Corrections.

O PLAY #90

You Have Assessed Why You Are Not Getting Enough Traffic and Have Made the Necessary Corrections.

O PLAY #91

You Have Assessed Why You Are Getting Calls From Potential Customers Outside Your Service Area and Have Made the Necessary Corrections.

SECTION 10

O PLAY #92

You Have Carefully Assessed Your Current PPC Management Contract And Know Exactly What Is Being Delivered.

O PLAY #93

You have access to a dashboard that reports the same information that you see in the billing statements from advertisers.

O PLAY #94

Your Provider Is Using the Latest Advertising Technology in Your Campaigns and Landing Pages to Improve Your Performance.

○ **PLAY #95**

Request A Change History Report From Your Provider That Details When Changes Happen In Your Account. You Have A Detailed Audit Trail That Supports Their Efforts.

○ **PLAY #96**

You Are Not Running The Same Ad Copy That Was Written When Your Account Was Created. They Are Testing Your Ads In The New Responsive Search Ads Format.

○ **PLAY #97**

You Have A Monthly Management Call Which Discusses Key Performance Metrics And A Plan To Address Underperforming Campaigns.

○ **PLAY #98**

Your PPC Manager Uses Individual Keyword Conversion To Track Your Success. They Have Implemented All Necessary Technical Aspects To Ensure Accuracy.

○ **PLAY #99**

You Are Billed Directly By Advertisers And Pay A Flat Rate Or Ad Spend Percentage To Your PPC Manager.

○ **PLAY #100**

You Meet With Your PPC Manager Bi-Monthly Or Monthly. Changes Are Made In Reasonable Time Frames.

○ **PLAY #101**

Ask Your PPC Manager How Many Years Of Experience They Have And The Total Ad Spend They Manage In A Year.

"I never left the field saying I could have done more to get ready and that gives me piece of mind."

- Peyton Manning
(Chicken Parm You Taste so Good)

About The Author

Steve Teneriello
Google AdWords Lead Generation and Conversion Specialist

Steve Teneriello is a local lead generation expert and Founder of AdMachines- a Boston based Google Premier Pay-Per-Click Agency that helps local businesses throughout the US and Canada develop, implement, and manage hand-crafted lead generation campaigns.

His original book, *The Google AdWords Survival Guide*, helped local business owners go from just barely surviving to thriving with their pay-per-click marketing. Today, the pay-per-click landscape has changed and with more than 20 years of experience running pay-per-click lead generation campaigns as a Google Certified PPC Specialist Steve helps you navigate your way through the most current form of Google Ads in *The Pay-Per-Click Playbook*.

Steve is married to his amazing wife Alli and has two children, Madeline and William. He lives with his family in Newburyport, Massachusetts. When he isn't working, Steve enjoys fishing in the local river, watching Patriots football, and playing the trumpet.